THE BAREFOOT BOOK

The Barefoot Book
Economically appropriate services for the rural poor

Edited and introduced
by
Marilyn Carr

Intermediate Technology Publications 1989

Practical Action Publishing Ltd
The Schumacher Centre
Bourton on Dunsmore, Rugby,
Warwickshire CV23 9QZ, UK
www.practicalactionpublishing.org

© Intermediate Technology Publications 1989.

First published 1989\Digitised 2013

ISBN 10: 1 85339 014 3
ISBN 13: 9781853390142
ISBN Library Ebook: 9781780441719
Book DOI: http://dx.doi.org/10.3362/9781780441719

All rights reserved. No part of this publication may be reprinted or reproduced or utilized in any form or by any electronic, mechanical, or other means, now known or hereafter invented, including photocopying and recording, or in any information storage or retrieval system, without the written permission of the publishers.

A catalogue record for this book is available from the British Library.

The authors, contributors and/or editors have asserted their rights under the Copyright Designs and Patents Act 1988 to be identified as authors of this work.

Since 1974, Practical Action Publishing (formerly Intermediate Technology Publications and ITDG Publishing) has published and disseminated books and information in support of international development work throughout the world. Practical Action Publishing is a trading name of Practical Action Publishing Ltd (Company Reg. No. 1159018), the wholly owned publishing company of Practical Action. Practical Action Publishing trades only in support of its parent charity objectives and any profits are covenanted back to Practical Action (Charity Reg. No. 247257, Group VAT Registration No. 880 9924 76).

CONTENTS

Acknowledgements			(vi)
1	Introduction	Marilyn Carr	1
2	Doctors in China — the origins of the barefoot approach	Katherine Elliott	4
3	Vets in Nepal and India — the provision of barefoot animal health services	David Hadrill	14
4	Lawyers in Bangladesh — an experiment in legal literacy	Salma Sobhan	20
5	Economists in Ecuador and Nepal — the barefoot approach to rural development planning	Andrew Scott	29
6	Bankers in Bangladesh — giving credit where credit is due	Ken Marshall	38
7	Management Consultants in Kenya — the provision of barefoot business services	Malcolm Harper	49
8	Village Artisans in Botswana — the training of barefoot technicians	David Inger	57
9	Mechanics in India — Village-level handpump maintenance in action	Sanjit Roy	63
10	Builders in Iran, Guinea and the Sudan — the barefoot approach to shelter	John Norton	71
11	Geologists in Sri Lanka — the barefoot approach to natural resource development	Michael Katz	81
12	Lessons learned	Marilyn Carr	88

Tables

I	Ratio of vets to livestock units in selected countries	14
II	Loan record of Zamiran	39
III	Popular businesses for borrowers	45
IV	Experiences in barefoot business consultancy services	53
V	Characteristics of handpump mechanics in Ajmer District, Rajasthan	66
VI	Three-Tier and One-Tier Systems: A socio-economic comparison	68
VII	Three-Tier and One-Tier Systems: A technical comparison	69
VIII	Some examples of useful village mineral and energy resources	87

INTRODUCTION
Marilyn Carr

One key theme of the Appropriate Technology movement is that of helping people to help themselves, thus enabling them to contribute to the social and economic development of their communities and the nation as a whole.

Illustrations of this approach are generally made in terms of introducing improved equipment such as grinding mills, ploughs, pumps and looms to poor rural producers. Much less is written about ways and means of providing the services which rural communities need to work themselves out of poverty on a sustained basis.

The concept of 'intermediate' services, as opposed to 'intermediate' technology, is best known in its application to primary health care. It was in China that the now famous 'barefoot doctor' scheme was initiated in response to the government's promise to provide some type of health care to everyone. People from rural communities were chosen by their fellows and trained to provide basic health services. They were responsible to their communities and were paid by them and they formed the basis of a nationwide network of health care reaching the majority of China's population of 500 million — a feat which clearly would have been beyond the abilities of the country's 20,000 Western-trained doctors and 500,000 Chinese medical practitioners.

This decentralized, labour-intensive, low-cost, community-based approach to providing at least some health care facilities in rural areas has fired the imagination of development planners and practitioners around the world. It has been demonstrated in scores of countries with millions of poor people that, when enabled to do so, they themselves can solve many of their own health problems and make available a service they would otherwise have been denied.

However, health care is only one of the basic services needed to help rural dwellers. Communities also need access to veterinary services to help care for their livestock, assistance with legal and administrative matters, advice on running a business or building a house, and maintenance and repair service for pumps and other village equipment.

It is known that it would be impossible to provide such services to large numbers of rural communities using highly trained professionals. The cost of training professional vets, lawyers, business consultants, engineers and architects is so great that their numbers will always be limited in relation to the numbers of people who need their advice and assistance. In any case, the system of which they are part is better suited to the needs and circumstances of the urban and rural rich than to those of the masses of the the rural poor. Their fees are high, their knowledge is very specialized and they tend to be located in cities and major towns — all factors which limit their usefulness to the majority of the population.

This does not mean that rural communities have to be denied access to all assistance. As the following chapters show, there is a growing number of examples of the decentralized, community-controlled approach to the provision of a wide range of services. Although these examples show that the 'intermediate' approach can be just as successful in the provision of these other services as it has been in the provision of primary health care, it has been much less widely publicized.

It is hoped that by drawing some of the available case studies together, this book will bring the value of the approach to the attention of the policy makers and development practitioners who can assist in the process of its widespread application. Only then will the masses of the rural poor have access to the services they need for a better quality of life, at a price they can afford.

A book of this nature would be incomplete without something on 'barefoot doctors' and the chapter by Katherine Elliott sets the context by examining the 'barefoot' approach in its original application. This is followed by David Hadrill's account of 'barefoot vets' in Nepal and India, where traditional healers and the livestock owners themselves have been trained in improved techniques of animal health care.

The next two chapters relate to the provision of legal and administrative services in rural communities. Salma Sobhan writes about the experience of training selected members of rural communities in Bangladesh to be paralegals who provide advice on family, land, inheritance and constitutional law to their neighbours. This is followed by an account of attempts in Ecuador and Nepal to enable rural communities to be involved in the planning and administration of their own development. The author, Andrew Scott, uses these examples to explore the meaning of 'barefoot economists' in the Third World.

The next three chapters deal with services related to the ability of rural communities to engage in profitable manufacturing and commercial enterprise. Ken Marshall's chapter on 'barefoot bankers' describes the experience of the now famous Grameen Bank in Bangladesh which lends to thousands of rural landless — the majority of whom are women. The chapter by Malcolm Harper examines experiences from Kenya and elsewhere in providing management consultancy services to rural entrepreneurs, and David Inger's chapter on village artisans in Botswana examines the experience of *Rural Industries Promotions* in training 'barefoot technicians'. Each of these chapters emphasizes a different type of assistance to small enterprise — credit, business advice and technical training.

The following three chapters cover three quite separate but very interesting applications of the 'barefoot' approach. Sanjit Roy describes an example of the provision of maintenance services for village-level equipment — the 'barefoot handpump mechanics' of Rajasthan State in India. John Norton looks at the 'barefoot' approach to shelter and describes programmes which have upgraded the skills of traditional builders and introduced basic knowledge of building techniques to community workers in various parts of the world. Geologists are the subject of Michael Katz's chapter which examines the 'barefoot' approach to natural resource development by which rural communities are enabled to identify and conserve the resources around them.

The final chapter tries to draw some general conclusions from the various case studies and provides recommendations on how 'intermediate' services can reach even greater numbers of rural communities.

DOCTORS IN CHINA — THE ORIGINS OF THE BAREFOOT APPROACH
Katherine Elliott

> When Health is absent
> Wisdom cannot reveal itself
> Art cannot become manifest,
> Strength cannot fight,
> Wealth becomes useless
> And Intelligence cannot be applied

These words were written more than two thousand years ago by Herophilus, a Greek physician who lived in Alexandria. They were echoed by Florence Nightingale in the latter half of the nineteenth century when she suggested that 'Health is not only to be well but to be able to use well every power that we have to use'. Today's World Health Organization aims for 'complete physical, mental and social well-being'.

The concept of health does not change with the passing of time, merely the phraseology. Health is at the central core of the process of development because development is essentially about people and the circumstances in which they live, work, play and reproduce themselves. It is, according to the dictionary, a process of advancement or opening up through successive stages to a more complex or mature state. Development implies a working out, an unfolding of potentialities. Through development, people come to exert greater control over their environment for their own benefit; they begin to escape from hunger and from dangerous communicable diseases; they lead fuller lives with education and access to knowledge. Increased well-being for the people should be implicit in all approaches to development planning, and better health must be among the earliest objectives.

Curiously, people mostly seem to take health for granted, although they want to receive medical care when they are ill or injured. In less developed countries, it has to be remembered that years and generations of poverty and deprivation may mean that the people are not aware of how it feels to enjoy their full health potential. They lack energy and sometimes the optimism that goes with that energy. They may feel trapped within a vicious circle of poor circumstances from which they cannot see how to escape, since all they seem to be able to do is just to survive from day to day. If people in such a situation are asked about what they need most, they hardly ever talk about health. Instead, they wish for work opportunities, for better food and houses and for education for their children. After those wishes, the need for medicines for the sick may come next. Yet food and housing, education and earning capacity are all very much involved with the standards of health enjoyed by the people of any country. This intersectoral effect needs to be remembered in planning for the maximum benefit from scarce resources for development.

There is, it seems, a distinction in the minds of most people between health and the care of the sick. This is important when it comes to consideration of the shape of a health care service which will be most useful to a community. Curative medicine is only one aspect of health care and there are other preventive and positive health components that can have a far greater impact on community health than conventional hospital-based medicine. These are often ignored by the community.

Inappropriate western health systems

The health needs of people in poorer parts of the world are not being met by health care systems based on curative western models (and some cynics might say that many western health care systems are failing to meet the real health needs of most people wherever they live!). There are still places where people are born, live out their often too brief lives and die without ever having access to modern medical care in any shape or form. Also, most developing countries have, in the past, modelled their health services along western lines — that is, they have tried to provide care based on the use of highly trained health professionals who are accustomed to working in high technology settings, such as hospitals and well equipped clinics. Such professionals are costly to train and they seldom function well outside the city or large town. In developed countries, communications are good and there is no great problem about people travelling to centres of medical excellence. In poorer countries, communications are difficult, expensive and sometimes non-existent. Yet in poorer countries, a large proportion of the population remains rural, although this situation is gradually changing with the drift to the cities and the resulting vast increase in urban slums and surrounding shanty towns. Needless to say, urbanization brings its own health problems and the plight of the urban poor may be even greater than that of the rural poor.

It has been clear for several decades that new approaches to the delivery of health care for those most in need — the poor, the deprived and the overlooked — had to be found everywhere; and that, in a shrinking crowded world, the time left to accomplish this is brief. Drought, floods and famines recur with frightening regularity. Wars and civil unrest add to the toll of natural disasters, and all the time our communications expand and extend, bringing the sight of death from starvation into the living rooms of the more prosperous via real-time television. Simultaneously, it must not be forgotten that the communication media are not one-way mirrors. Transistor radios are everywhere in the Third World, and television screens in shop windows and in cheap bars and eating places are eagerly watched. The poorest of the poor in developing countries are now much more aware that alleviation of their miseries is possible, given the necessary resources. The vicious cycle of poverty, malnutrition, disease, ignorance and too many children being born to die in infancy can indeed be broken when people are given the tools, the knowledge, the goodwill and the incentives.

Health for all by the year 2000

The United Nations International Children's Emergency Fund (UNICEF) has its Child Survival programme. Encapsulated in the acronym: GOBI-FFF, efforts to improve child survival highlight important aspects of child health. GOBI stands for Growth monitoring; Oral rehydration treatment of acute diarrhoea; Breastfeeding for good infant nutrition and also protection against infection; and Immunization against the common communicable diseases of childhood. To these first four promotions, UNICEF quickly added the three Fs — Food, Family spacing and Female education, for without enough food children fail to grow and to resist infection. Children born to very young or to elderly mothers, too close together and too many in number are at extra risk themselves and they put their mothers at great risk. Many Third World women die from causes associated with pregnancy and childbirth (over half a million a year) and, for every woman who dies there are countless others whose health is depleted or grossly damaged. The health of a child is closely bound up with that of its mother, beginning at conception, and small children depend so much in their early years on the quality of care their mothers are able to provide. Family spacing and female education are essential components of any effort to improve family health and child survival.

UNICEF programmes in general and child survival programmes in particular have already shown what a lot can be done to save lives and improve health at community level, but the benefits tend to fade away unless responsibility for the programmes is accepted by the community.

At Alma Ata in 1978, the World Health Organization and UNICEF together set out the target of Health for All by the Year 2000, based on the concept of access by all to primary health care; and most governments pledged themselves to support the Declaration of Alma Ata. The World Health Organization, both before and since 1978, has done a great deal to promote the extension of basic health services throughout the developing world. Primary health care is basic health care at household and community level and includes the prevention of illness as well as its cure. Health education and environmental hygiene therefore play important roles in primary health care alongside the treatment of minor illnesses and injuries.

Development is about a better quality of life for people. A better quality of life should improve people's health but, looking at development the other way round, healthier people are able to do more for themselves towards improving the quality of life for themselves and their families. The largest resource available to most developing countries is people and it may well be that people can make a much greater contribution to their own health improvement than has ever been taken into the world reckoning of development resources.

Demystification of medicine

It has long been obvious that primary health care could never be provided on the scale required to meet the WHO/UNICEF target of Health for All by the Year 2000 if primary health care had to depend on the equitable deployment of trained health professionals. The then Director-General of the World Health Organization, Dr Halfdan Mahler, called more than 10 years ago for a 'demystification of medicine'. This was at a time when there was great interest in alternatives to full health professionals, people who were then classified as auxiliary health workers. This was not a new idea. It was one that had begun seriously among medical missionary services and colonial medical services as a form of apprenticeship to meet the obvious needs. Likely local people were picked to help out as attendants. In Fiji, for instance, the Medical School had been training local primary care practitioners since the end of the last century in a long and honourable tradition — and there were a number of similar examples elsewhere.

However, it was the news coming out of China towards the end of the 1960s about the 'barefoot doctors' who were part of Chairman Mao's 'cultural revolution' that brought the innovation in the health care delivery pot to the boil.

Lessons from China

China is an enormous country with a huge population and in 1950, at the time of Liberation, the new government recognized that it had few material resources to cope with a disease-ridden population living in an extremely unhealthy environment. It realized that there was no way in which China's problems could be solved by health care along western lines, using a hospital-based curative approach, high technology and highly trained and therefore expensive health professionals. National principles of health care were agreed covering four main areas for immediate action. These were: service to the people; disease prevention; integration of traditional and modern systems of health, both curative and preventive ('walking on two legs'); and mass campaigns involving everyone, not especially the doctors. These campaigns increased public awareness of health issues and led to widespread acceptance of the responsibility of individuals for their own health and for the health of the community.

During the 1950s and early 1960s, environmental improvement came about through the elimination of pests such as rats, flies, mosquitoes, bed bugs etc and with the introduction of improved sanitary facilities, which also controlled and made productive use of human wastes. There were specific programmes of action: vaccination against smallpox; elimination of sexually transmitted diseases; broader vaccination campaigns, including vaccination of all new-borns against tuberculosis; control of both malaria and schistosomiasis through mass case finding, treatment and environmental action against the vectors of these diseases. To carry out these programmes, auxiliary workers were specifically recruited and trained and the programmes received full support sociopolitically, including extensive use of the media.

Having, so to speak, cleaned up some of the most obvious and urgent health problems by the mid-1960s, the Chinese leadership, using the gathering forces of the Cultural Revolution, focused on the more personal health care needs of the population. Only about 20 per cent of the people lived in the urban areas, but this small percentage included almost all the professional medical personnel, leaving the vast majority of the population to their own devices, healthwise. One third of all health professionals were forthwith ordered to the rural areas and, for the next 10 years, either permanently or periodically, they provided health services to the villages in the shape of mobile medical teams. Coming face to face in this way (probably for the first time) with the massive health care problems of the vast majority of their countrymen had an interesting as well as a salutary effect on China's high-level medical academics and public health officials. The vast burden of ill health was impossible for them to handle on their own and they may also have felt that the work that was needed was to some extent a waste of their own expensively acquired skills. A rural health service had to be provided and the decision was made to recruit and train village-level health workers — barefoot doctors, or more literally from the Chinese term 'doctors without shoes'.

Initially the barefoot doctors were multipurpose health workers chosen by the mobile teams in conjunction with the communities to be served, and trained as near as possible to where they were to work, sometimes in short periods between times of intense agricultural activity since the barefoot doctors remained part of their communities and shared in the day-to-day work of the peasants. They had responsibility for preventive health care such as environmental improvement, vaccination and family planning. They also dealt with everyday illnesses and accidents and with pregnancy and delivery. They referred problems beyond their capability to the nearest medical centre. They seem to have had a very valuable impact on the health status of the Chinese rural people.

There is continuing education for barefoot doctors and career opportunities to the extent of eventual entry into medical school. It will be interesting to see how this trend changes the relationship between the barefoot doctors and their communities. Traditional and modern medicine in China appear to have been successfully integrated, resulting in an affordable system to meet the needs of everyone and also bringing some interesting scientific benefits, not only to China but to the rest of the world.

It seems, however, that China is now beginning to place greater stress on the value of more sophisticated technologies and on greater professionalization and medicalization of the health system. It would be sad if this new trend devalued the Chinese example because there is no doubt that, over the last 30 years,

China has managed to improve the health of the Chinese people significantly despite the low per capita income. Malnutrition has been eradicated, life expectancy raised to at least 65, and infant mortality and population growth rates substantially lowered. The whole system ought to be given the credit for this success, not just the barefoot doctors. Perhaps the most important lesson to be learned from China is that the barefoot doctor concept has succeeded because of the supportive political, socio-economic and administrative back-up it has received — and that without the commitment of all of the people to the development of an equitable health care system, health care workers of the 'barefoot' type are going to become easily discouraged and their communities disillusioned.

Factors in success

The Chinese experience has been studied and compared with many other interesting examples of alternative approaches to primary health care from different parts of the world. Certain points seem to be crucial in almost all situations: selection by whom; type and location of training; supervision and accountability; financing; equipment and drug supplies; referral possibilities; relationship with local traditional healers, if any; cultural considerations, such as the seclusion of women; the blend of curative and preventive care; intersectoral aspects, for example,, with agriculture, housing, education etc; promotion possibilities, if any, and the value of in-service training; methods of evaluation, and, last but not least, the need not to underestimate the value of the part-time health worker, as seen in the Chinese example, the Latin American *campesino* or *promotora de salud*, the Eskimo health aides and so on.

Now we mostly speak about community health workers and there is no longer any doubt that the full-time or the part-time community health worker can play a very significant part in dealing with health-related problems in any society. Their closeness to the society gives them greater understanding and, if well selected, useful influence and respect. All the points mentioned above are significant but it might be useful to elaborate on two: financing, and supervision and accountability.

Financing

Money is always important, even if it is in the form of some kind of barter system. The community health workers may gain status through their role but they also need to live and to have at least minimal equipment for their work. It appears, looking at the experience of many countries, that the more successful community health worker projects are those where the people contribute directly in some way. In the Chinese communes, the rate was fixed according to the earning capacity of each worker. If more was needed, it could be obtained from the government but there was pride in managing where they could.

In one interesting project in Indonesia, the community set up two funds: a development fund and a health fund, and people contributed to both according to their means. The development fund lent money for development. The health fund paid the health workers and bought medicines. Any shortfall in the health fund had to be made good by the development fund; any surplus was added to the development fund. This system meant that everyone kept a close watch on health costs and an open mind about ways to improve the health status of the community — for instance, with future savings to come from a safer water supply. Sad to say, it seems that where community health workers receive their pay from a distant government, they are seldom as industrious as those paid by the community.

Supervision and accountability

Supervision and accountability are both important as professional support for 'barefoot' health care personnel. All health care must be a team effort even though the team members may at times be widely separated. Through training, responsibility is delegated from teacher to pupil but the final accountability in health care cannot be delegated. The health professionals who train the community health workers must remain finally accountable for standards of care at community level. This entails regular supervision of their work to encourage as much as to correct, and also to add to their skills and to enhance their status within the community. Accountability means making sure that community-level health care workers are not left to struggle in isolation with problems which exceed their own competence, but for which they may be aware that a solution exists elsewhere.

It is certain that the 'barefoot doctor' will always have a place in all systems of health care. Since the human race began, there have always been people who helped with the health problems of others — the wise women, the bone-setters, the herbalists, the birth attendants, the healers — all had something that others recognized as valuable. Even among the most sophisticated societies, vestiges of this tradition remain and are now being fostered as conventional medical care realizes its limitations in the face of the myriad problems it faces, like violence and drug abuse and the social isolation of the handicapped and the elderly.

As Sigerist said more than 50 years ago, 'Health cannot be forced upon the people. It cannot be dispensed to the people. They must want it and be prepared to do their share and to co-operate fully in whatever health programme a country develops'. Ivan Illich put it more succinctly. 'Health is something people do, not something people get.' Development and health must go hand in hand, for one will not succeed without the other. The 'barefoot doctor' represents the importance for the future of the world that people everywhere should share the power of knowledge and expertise and use this new power to benefit others as well as themselves. According to the Chinese, 'Many little things done in many little places by many little people will change the face of the world' — and in no facet of development is this more true than in the vital facet of health.

VETS IN NEPAL AND INDIA — THE PROVISION OF BAREFOOT ANIMAL HEALTH SERVICES

David Hadrill

People living in the harshest environments, where crop production is difficult, depend on livestock for survival. In arid and mountainous regions, animals such as goats and yaks, sheep and camels graze scant vegetation and produce milk, meat, hides, wool and draught power, providing stock owners with a livelihood.

Where crops are cultivated in areas with a wetter tropical climate, draught animals have an extremely important role in tilling the land. It is estimated that of the 900 million cattle and buffaloes in developing countries, 250 to 300 million are used for draught purposes. Animal power is used for other important activities including transporting farm produce to the market and raising well water. Farmers need their draught animals to be fit, healthy and ready to work, particularly in areas with seasonal rainfall and a short growing season, where days lost can result in large reductions in crop yields.

Professional vets

In most poor countries, and especially in remote regions, adequate veterinary services are only available to a limited number of livestock owners. One reason for this is the shortage of vets in many developing countries. This is well illustrated in Table 1 which compares livestock to vet ratios in developed and developing countries.

The problem is compounded by the fact that most of the limited number of vets in developing countries are concentrated in urban and better-resourced rural areas. Thus, the poorest farmers in the remoter rural areas have very little likelihood of gaining access to a fully qualified vet.

Table 1: Ratio of vets to livestock units in selected countries

Country	Livestock Units LU ('000)	Vets	LU ('000) per vet
UK	16,896	6,216	2.7
Nepal	993	40	249.8
USA	127,261	30,371	4.2
India	222,860	10,800	20.6
Kenya	7,560	186	40.6
Ethiopia	32,373	104	31.3

Source: FAO/WHO, 1979.

It has been recognized for some time that it is neither feasible nor desirable for poor countries to emulate the rich countries' veterinary system by attempting to train equivalent numbers of vets. It is very expensive to build Veterinary Schools, run the courses and then pay salaries and provide vehicles to vets after graduation. Therefore, in most developing countries a paraprofessional cadre known as Animal Health Assistants or AHAs has been added to the state veterinary service.

Animal Health Assistants (AHAs)

The training for an AHA is considerably shorter than the full course, usually lasting two years. An example of a well-established institution giving training at this level is the Animal Health and Industry Training Institute at Kabele near Nairobi, and AHAs now constitute an integral part of the Kenyan state veterinary service. For each vet there are several AHAs working in contact with livestock owners, thus extending the range of work of the nearest Veterinary Officer. They are able to report outbreaks of serious disease to the vet and treat routine cases unsupervised.

Although AHAs have helped fill gaps, areas remain where farmers and herdsmen have no trained representative of the veterinary service to turn to when their livestock falls sick. In these circumstances farmers throughout the developing world treat their animals themselves or else seek advice from local traditional healers, some of whom treat both animals and people. Farmers often buy veterinary medicines (though by law these drugs may be available by prescription only) without accurate knowledge of the conditions for which the drugs are prescribed or their correct doses and storage. Some local healers have picked up knowledge of the applications of particular modern medicines, but frequently they rely on traditional methods which include the use of local medicinal plants and some techniques of dubious value like the placation of evil spirits or chanting *mantras*.

Community Animal Health Workers

In several countries, non-governmental organizations have initiated programmes in under-resourced areas to upgrade local knowledge about what action to take when an animal falls sick, by training animal health workers within the community. A major advantage of training local people, preferably those who own stock themselves, is that they are likely to have a strong allegiance to the livestock-owning members of their own community and a genuine desire to work with and for them. After training as animal health workers their status increases and in most cases they are content to provide a service in return for favours, the respect of their neighbours and a nominal income.

By contrast, the AHA's allegiance is usually to the hierarchy of the State Veterinary Service. When a job with more attractive terms and conditions becomes available elsewhere, the AHA may leave. Animal health worker training programmes are established in many countries. Examples from Nepal and India are described below.

Nepal's animal health improvement programme

In the Nepali Himalayas, villagers who had been in contact with the United Mission to Nepal (UMN) Community Health projects made requests for help with livestock health. Following visits by a British vet, Alison Craven, the 'Animal Health Improvement Programme' was planned and the full programme began in 1981.

The programme aims to provide training to selected villagers so that they will be able to examine a sick animal and treat it or refer it to a veterinary hospital if there is one nearby. It also aims to educate farmers in improved animal husbandry techniques so that common diseases are prevented. From 1981 to 1986, 256 village farmers and 43 UMN staff were trained as village Animal Health Workers in intensive two-week residential courses. All courses are given in the winter when farmers in Nepal are not busy on the land.

Three or four classes are given each year: one or two for beginners, one for those who had difficulties during or after the first course, and an advanced course for those who are working well or who will be UMN supervisory staff. All courses are held at the farm at the UMN's Rural Development Centre near Pokhara.

The programme organizers have found it beneficial to carry out training at the Centre rather than in villages because the farm has its own animals which can be used during courses for practising techniques such as restraint and foot trimming. Additionally, sick animals are brought to the Centre's clinic by local people throughout the year, thus enabling the demonstration of examination and treatment of clinical cases.

The trainees come from many rural areas in Nepal. Initial contact has usually been made through one of UMN's other programmes. The community is involved with the selection of a trainee animal health worker and is encouraged to choose a mature farmer who is respected and who has a genuine interest in animals rather than a young well-educated man who would be more likely to be attracted away from his village by more lucrative employment elsewhere. It is considered essential that the trainees are able to read and write Nepali.

To help the trainees to remember factual material they are given leaflets written in Nepali which cover topics such as doses of medicines. At the end of the course, there are short written and practical tests to check their understanding. In the refresher course, the subjects covered in the basic course are revised, poisoning and some new diseases are discussed, problems which have arisen since the basic course are dealt with and the animal health workers practise preparing and presenting a short talk, with the intention that they will organize meetings for other farmers when they return to their villages.

At present the expatriate UMN staff visit the trainees once or twice a year in their villages. This is an opportunity to discuss progress, and advise and encourage. The responsibility for follow-up is increasingly being given to local people who have attended one of the courses. Local supervisors in each area ensure more frequent contact and facilitate medicine distribution and the rapid communication of problems back to the Centre.

Trainees are instructed in the use of only those veterinary drugs which are readily available in Nepal. However, drugs cannot always be obtained in remote hill areas and at present the programme supplies them. In the long term it is hoped that local shops will stock these medicines.

The community has to decide how to remunerate the trained farmers for their services as village Animal Health Worker. Often the basic box of drugs is provided free initially with instructions to sell at 10 per cent profit and to use the cash to maintain stocks.

However, difficulties arise when treating animals belonging to friends or relatives who may not feel they should pay. Sometimes payment in kind or in food is made. Programme staff may have to hold a meeting in the community and point out that if the medicines are not paid for, the supplies will be exhausted and the service will cease. It is sometimes also necessary to persuade the trainees to save the money collected for buying more medicines.

In general, the programme has achieved significant results because of the UMN staffs' capability and strong commitment and the eagerness to learn shown by the Nepali farmers, who frequently had to deal with their animal problems themselves since many of them live several days walk from the nearest veterinary facility.

Upgrading traditional veterinary skills in India

A somewhat different approach to training Animal Health Workers has been developed in Kutch in western India where herdsmen and *deshis* (local animal doctors), most of whom are illiterate, are trained for just three days in the use of a 'PACK' or Primary Animal Health Care Kit. The kit contains basic veterinary equipment and 10 medicines obtainable from local chemist shops.

Kutch has an arid to semi-arid climate and much of the land area is either rough grazing or barren. Keeping livestock is an important activity for many Kutchi people and yet out of 26 government veterinary posts only 12 were filled in 1986. A local rural development organization, the Vivekanand Research and Training Institute (VRTI) first worked with Kutchi stock owners during a massive sheep and goat deworming and vaccination campaign as part of relief work during a period of drought. From this involvement grew the desire to establish a long-term livestock development project.

Within the livestock-owning communities in Kutch there are people known as *deshis* — doctors who treat sick human and animal patients. These people usually give treatments free of charge, but the nature of their work means that they are well respected and they have a high status.

When starting its livestock development project, VRTI identified experienced *deshi* animal doctors and discussed with them major local livestock problems and the sorts of treatments they used. VRTI personnel found that the *deshis* could clearly describe and give local names to many diseases, but there were some conditions which did not respond favourably to any of their treatments.

Their concepts of the causes and transmission of diseases and how to prevent them were vague. From these discussions and VRTI's own knowledge, the topics for an initial primary animal health care course were selected. Medicines and equipment were chosen for a kit to help extend the range of disease that local people could treat effectively and a training programme was prepared.

Training consists of a short, participative course carried out on three separate days, with a week or more between each day's training. Instead of a residential course at a training centre this training is conducted near to the homes of the trainees so that poor livestock farmers, who may not be able to leave home for a residential course, are not excluded from training.

Selection of trainees followed many visits and discussions by VRTI field staff. In most villages selection was easy because there was one herdsman or *deshi* who performed most of the treatments. In other communities there were many meetings with farmers known to VRTI staff, village leaders and others before choosing candidates for the PACK course. Before training began, meetings were always held with the *sarpanch*, the leader of the village council and, where possible, a mass meeting was held to inform as many people as possible of the new service.

An important feature of the training methodology employed is the emphasis on participative techniques and learning practical skills by supervised practice. Instructional techniques developed by the British Agricultural Training Board were adapted for use in Kutch. In particular, VRTI trainers were shown how to use question and answer techniques effectively to involve all members of the group and maintain their concentration without exposing an individual's lack of knowledge; how to plan for training (including the production of illustrated leaflets for trainees, many of whom were illiterate); and how to instruct people in new practical skills, building their confidence and competence in carrying out new tasks.

The basic kit of drugs and equipment which is provided to the Animal Health Workers during their training (the cost of a PACK is about Rs.150 or £7) is paid for by VRTI from its own funds. However, during training it is stressed that treatments must be recorded and charged for according to recommended fees. If the PACK holder is illiterate, a literate neighbour or relative writes in the case book the condition observed and the treatment given. On the 28th of each month all Animal Health Workers come to VRTI's office (bus fares are paid for those who have far to come) and bring their case books with the previous month's entries. The

PACKs are restocked from VRTI's store of medicines purchased from local chemist shops. The Animal Health Workers have to pay for replacement medicines although VRTI has been subsidizing the cost by 50 per cent. This has been justified because *deshi*-doctors formerly worked without charging for their services and have difficulty in recouping the money. Ideally, in the future, village shops will stock PACK medicines and Animal Health Workers will charge enough to buy replacement medicines directly. Because *deshi*-doctors have worked in the past without cash payment, the cost-recovery component of the system, which is fundamental to the eventual independence and self-reliance of the Animal Health Workers, has proved difficult to achieve.

Mass meetings to inform villagers of the existence of the PACK service and to emphasize the terms on which it is provided have helped the people to realize that if they want the service to continue it must be paid for. Some had thought that all medicines were free or that the Animal Health Workers were paid salaries by VRTI. Most people know that if the 'Veterinary Doctor' is called from the town a considerable charge will be incurred and are slow to accept that the Animal Health Worker must be paid too if he or she is to be able to restock the kit. The Animal Health Workers themselves now clearly understand that when they come for replacement medicines at the end of the month they must pay for them.

The system has been well accepted by the authorities. This is partly due to VRTI's connections and good relations with local dignitaries, but also because the government vet based in the town in the project area has found that the project does not encroach on his work. Since the cases treated by Animal Health Workers mainly belong to poor farmers in villages far from the town, the vet is relieved not to be burdened with the extra work load.

By 1986, 18 PACK centres were operational and in the preceding two years almost 4,000 cases had been treated by Animal Health Workers.

The success of the animal health programme in Kutch has encouraged the uptake of the method by other development agencies in different locations in Gujarat State.

In addition, the Intermediate Technology Development Group has employed a vet to establish related livestock development work in Kenya, where a similar decentralized approach to training will upgrade local skills in a way designed to be of long-lasting value to the livestock-owning community.

LAWYERS IN BANGLADESH — AN EXPERIMENT IN LEGAL LITERACY

Salma Sobhan

Sample case histories

In Nandar Ali's village a young man was about to be married. The young man's parents, as has become customary in recent years, were demanding a dowry from the bride's family. Nandar Ali explained to the parents that the giving or taking of a dowry is against the law. The parents were not convinced, but Nandar Ali did not give up. He approached the young man himself who proved to be more easily persuaded and agreed to a dowryless marriage. The young man's parents were incensed but he remained adamant and the marriage took place without a dowry. His father refused to attend the wedding but a week later was seen to be 'coming round'.

Hashim is arranging for the registration of a marriage. He has contacted the marriage registrar for that area and made it clear to him that he knows the official rates for the registrar's services. The registrar understands that he must comply with these. The parents of the couple are reassured that the cost of complying with the legal provisions that make registration of a marriage mandatory will not be prohibitive. The bride's parents in particular feel reassured that the terms and conditions of the marriage are to be documented. This will not make the marriage any more stable but it will at least impress upon the groom and his family that they are committed to certain duties. If there is any marital dispute, the registration document will give the bride access to the courts.

'Munshi', as he is known in the village, is respected for being an educated man (the literal meaning of munshi is scribe — 'Munshi's' name is Queyamuddin). People often come to him to solemnize marriages. Under the Marriage Registration Act, only the duly appointed Marriage Registrars can *register* a marriage. Although these officials can also solemnize marriages, 'non-officials' are not barred from doing so. Munshi is approached by the parents of a young girl and asked to officiate at her marriage. Munshi asks how old the girl is. The parents say 'about 16 or 17 years old'. Munshi tells them that their daughter is under age — the minimum age for marriage for girls in Bangladesh is 18 — and that they should wait till she is of marriageable age.

Sonaban hears from her neighbour that a marriage has been arranged in the village on the payment of a dowry. Sonaban goes to the bride's parents and explains to them that, under the law, they are punishable if they give a dowry to their daughter. The punishment is a year's imprisonment, she tells them, or a heavy fine, or even both.

Nandar Ali, Hashim, Munshi and Sonaban are four members of a group who are known as paralegals. This group is the first of its kind — a gathering of lay, mostly unlettered villagers who have, over a period of nine months, received training from the Bangladesh Rural Advancement Committee (BRAC) in some aspects of the law. There are altogether 18 of them, ten women and eight men, with ages ranging from 32 to 56, and they are the vanguard of an exciting experiment in legal literacy.

Bangladesh Rural Advancement Committee

The Bangladesh Rural Advancement Committee (BRAC) is an organization that works with the rural poor. Its target groups are made up of those villagers who have to sell their labour for more than 100 days in a year. BRAC has been functioning since 1972 and it quickly moved out of the relief work that was necessary in the aftermath of the war in 1971 into development work. It aims at self-sufficiency and works towards 'involving the rural people themselves in the planning process to enhance their power to change the traditional relationships of dependency and to increase their control over productive resources'. The groups are trained to identify problems and their sources and to try to work towards solutions. Integrated programmes have been developed dealing with health and nutrition, management (human development and communications), primary and adult education and income-generation schemes. There is a continuous evaluation process in keeping with BRAC's philosophy of learning from its mistakes. Outside evaluations are also invited.

One such evaluation, carried out in 1983, recommended that 'a future need for village women (as well as village men) is legal support services. Some ways this could be done is by training paralegal workers to operate in the villages, by lobbying for government legal information centres and by educating members of the resourceless women's groups as legal workers who would teach women their legal rights and have some working knowledge of the Court system'. This was a need of which BRAC workers themselves were becoming increasingly aware, and so the decision to introduce a Paralegal Training Programme was reached. This programme, in keeping with established practice, was developed in conjunction with the target groups.

Surveys and salishes

Certain data had to be collected to identify those situations which give rise to conflict in the rural areas. Thus it was decided that two surveys would be undertaken. One survey would be held in an area where BRAC was active and another in an area where BRAC was not working. In addition, it was decided it would be useful to find out how well the *salish* worked.

Disputes are settled in the villages by the calling of a *salish* — a gathering of the village elders and élite who hear both sides and pronounce a judgment. The *salish* is popularly supposed to be an effective forum for dispute settlement. It is quick, since the disputing parties do not have to waste time and money in travelling to the nearest court and paying lawyers, and the 'Judges' are local people who know the general background.

Whether or not the *salish* has ever functioned as well as is supposed is debatable, but over the years the institution appears to have fallen into disrepute. One hears complaints that it is used by the richer and more influential members of society to keep the poor in line. It is difficult to get a *salish* constituted to hear a particular grievance unless one has the right connections. There is no guarantee that any known rules will prevail and there is little chance that a powerful disputant will abide by a decision that is against his own interests.

The surveys confirmed these complaints. It appeared that less than one third of disputes were referred to a *salish*. Quite often the narrator of the grievance would say 'I have no connections, so I was not able to get a *salish* called.' Out of those cases which were referred to the *salish* for settlement, the decision was often ignored by the losing party.

Despite this, it seemed a pity that the *salish* should lose credibility, and one of the aims of paralegal training was to see if the paralegals could work to make it a more effective forum.

The role of the paralegal

The term paralegal in the context of the BRAC programme is misleading. There is a tendency to equate paralegal personnel with paramedical personnel. A paramedic however has the great advantage of being able to be effective on two fronts — prevention and cure. By contrast, a paralegal's ability to effect a legal cure is very limited. Therefore it was decided that the objectives of the paralegal training would be to train people to inform others of their legal rights and to try to gain access to the *salish* where it was hoped that they would be in a position to make an informed input.

Thus, of the four possible roles that a paralegal could play as:
○ repositories and disseminators of information
○ counsellors, advisers and arbiters
○ Intervenors, 'watchdogs' and
○ conduits to and liaison with the legal profession,
it was decided to limit the scope of their functions to the first two.

Recruitment and training

Twenty of the target groups were informed that BRAC would be starting a paralegal training programme and were asked to nominate a group member who would benefit from this training. The only guidelines were that the person should not be too involved with other BRAC programmes as this programme would need a considerable input of time. Their selections were excellent. There were only two drop-outs from the 20 selected and all the 18 appeared to have a natural aptitude for the law.

The first meeting with the paralegals was in August 1986. Tabulations of the two surveys on issues giving rise to conflict had shown that land and dowry caused the most problems. However, in keeping with BRAC's method of participatory teaching, the paralegal trainees were engaged in a dialogue about the issues on which they felt they most needed information.

This dialogue was very animated and everyone had a lot to say. Altogether about 20 issues or problems were identified. These ranged from dowry, maintenance and divorce to auction sales, inheritance rights and false arrest. On the basis of this dialogue three broad heads were identified — family law, inheritance and land law. (Later, a fourth module was added on constitutional law and criminal procedure.)

Each training class was scheduled to take place independently at intervals of at least six weeks and was to last for three to five days. Apart from the two trainers, who had in the preceding months received an intensive briefing in the law, there were five lawyers on the teaching team. These were the programme head and two researchers, (all three of whom were women) and the field back-up team.

The teaching modules were developed on the basis of the survey results but their structure was kept flexible to be able to incorporate the questions and problems of the class.

Family law

Discussions had been planned on the following topics: minimum age of marriage, the elements of a valid marriage, registration of marriages, polygamy, divorce, maintenance and the custody of children. A start was made by asking each of the paralegals details of their dates of marriage, their ages at the time and so on. Most of the men had been married in their early twenties, most of the women in their very early teens. It was possible to establish that the system of giving a dowry at the time of the marriage is a recent custom. All the paralegals said 'This did not happen in our time.' While everyone deplored it, they all agreed that it was difficult to avoid giving a dowry nowadays if one had daughters.

There was a general consensus that this had come from an imitation of the richer classes. According to them, the rich had started giving lavish gifts to the grooms of their daughters both from a vulgar desire to impress and because they had to get their less well-favoured daughters off their hands. What started as imitation had become an expectation and now it was a *sine qua non*. The class had only heard very vaguely that some law had been passed against the giving of dowries (Dowry Act 1981). They quickly made themselves acquainted with the details.

Polygamy and unilateral irrevocable divorce needed careful handling. The right of husbands in respect of both polygamy and divorce has been modified by statute law since 1961 but, whereas polygamy is rare, unilateral irrevocable divorce remains the most common form of divorce in the rural areas. The checks on a husband's right to 'put away' his wife were discussed. The fact that women had the right to initiate divorce proceedings and even exercise the right of unilateral divorce if this was written into their contracts was information that trainees received for the first time.

It was necessary during this training and the following one (on inheritance) to emphasize that the objectives of the statutory modifications were to reinforce the objectives of the Shariah law (which governs personal status laws for Muslims in Bangladesh).

Inheritance

The training on inheritance was a revelation. As the target group was virtually landless, it had seemed that the inheritance law would hardly be a topic of much interest. However, in the initial dialogue it was very clear that the paralegals felt that inheritance was a big issue, with the woman's share causing the most controversy: brothers dispossessed sisters, uncles their nieces, and so on. The Muslim law of inheritance is a complex mathematical exercise involving fractions, and fractions of fractions. The training was started by teaching the basics — who the primary claimants were and what their share was. One of the objectives here was to bring home the point that women were constituted heirs. This point was quickly picked up. It was already common knowledge that a wife inherited from her husband and the precise fraction of his estate that was her entitlement was known too. It had been planned to keep the training within these basics — quite complicated enough — but it proved impossible to satisfy the thirst for information, partly because the paralegals had personal problems which needed to be solved.

Ishaq Ali was interested in finding out whether he could claim a share in property belonging to his father's maternal grandmother. His father had not claimed a share and was now dead. What were Ishaq Ali's rights?

Zobeida's husband, who was one of four brothers, had bought out his brothers' shares in the inheritance which their father had left. His sister did not sell her share to him. What is her right?

Shonaban is the only child of her father who is dead. He predeceased his father, her grandfather, who has now also died. What are her rights to inherit from her father and grandfather?

These personal problems were marvellous teaching exercises and helped the trainers to see, as no amount of research would have done, the perspectives held by the people for whom the teaching programmes were being developed.

Land law

The training on land law was in a way the most important. The surveys showed that ownership and possession of land is the most crucial facet of life in the countryside.

The training here concentrated on practical procedures. One of the most common problems is that of the fraudulent deed. Property is transferred by sale, the buyer receives an impressive deed and fails to verify it. After money has changed hands and the seller has disappeared, the buyer finds himself in difficulties.

The training for this module was undertaken both in the classroom and in the offices to which it is necessary to go to verify title or to ascertain the precise boundaries of one's land. It was found that theoretically most of the men knew what had to be done. Khalil Bhai, who was the oldest trainee, gave the class a model answer on what he would do to verify a title. None of them had ever bothered to go through these motions, particularly in respect of any land they had inherited and were in possession of, because they said it was too expensive. They had not realized how vulnerable they were to a fraud being perpetrated against them.

It was soon made clear that the paralegals were misinformed about registration fees and so on. The amounts payable were not as exorbitant as they had been led to believe by the village 'touts' who offer to perform these tasks for a 'modest' fee, inflating the cost to increase their fee. The 'touts' offers had been refused but many registrations had not been made. The exercise also showed up the practice of letting others go to pay one's taxes without ever checking that it had been done, or the very dangerous practice of thumb-printing a blank piece of paper when someone offers to write out an application on another's behalf. All such practices were discouraged with examples of how such situations could be exploited.

Constitutional law and criminal procedure

The authority given to the police is unfortunately frequently misused and this, except where it is flagrant, is accepted by most villagers as the policeman's right. It was felt that it would be a useful exercise to discuss the powers and privileges of the police against the backdrop of the constitution, with particular emphasis on fundamental rights. It was also hoped that this would tackle the problem of the 'punishments' sometimes dictated by the *salish*.

Practice

The first training class was held in August 1986, the concluding class in May 1987. The interval between sessions was about two months. These intervals were used by the paralegals to hold meetings with their group members and also to approach people on an individual basis to pass on the information they had acquired. The lawyers in the field had to keep a very low profile. They were there solely to provide a back-up service to the paralegals in order to reinforce the training. They were not to correct paralegals publicly, even if they made mistakes, as to do so would have lessened their credibility and made the villagers turn directly to the lawyers for information. As it happened, the paralegals made few mistakes, only occasionally forgetting a point. Refresher sessions were then held with two or three of the paralegals who were having the same problem.

Evaluation

One of the things the trainers most wanted to learn was what the villagers thought of the paralegals and how they viewed the legal information they were passing on. The programme officers in the field were asked to give their own overall impressions of the performance of the paralegals and the impact of their teaching, and also to interview different sections of the community, including the village 'élite', who might be expected to resent this 'encroachment' on their preserves. The paralegals themselves were asked about their own impressions of their abilities and how they found themselves received.

There appeared to be an overall consensus in favour of the objectives of the programme. The paralegals themselves, from the first day of the training, said that this acquisition of knowledge had benefited them. Their litany was 'we didn't know these things and now we do'. This too was the refrain of those villagers who had attended the group meetings. The villagers however were a little sceptical about the outcome of all this learning. With regard to the anti-dowry law they said 'These laws are all very well, but we don't see them being enforced. Unless people are punished nothing will come of this.' They also commented that those who might already have been presumed to know the laws (the 'élite') were not particularly law-abiding. Some villagers who had disputes with members of the paralegals' families were a little sceptical as to the role those paralegals would play if they were called to attend a *salish* on those disputes.

As the months have gone by, the paralegals have become surer of themselves. The community knows more about them and feels that if community members can be trained in legal matters, they are not such esoteric affairs. The paralegal programme has gone a long way towards 'demystifying' the law.

Modifications of the programme

It was decided at the end of the first training to condense the four modules into two, because the paralegals could ill-afford to lose 25 working days in a year. This will mean that the modules themselves will have to be restructured to give them a logical structure.

The BRAC target groups will make the decision at their meetings as to whether the paralegals should receive any reimbursement for practical help they give. If a decision to pay them is made, the BRAC rule of collecting money from members and collectively reimbursing the paralegal for the service will have to be followed. Particular care will have to be taken to see that there is nothing resembling a lawyer/client relationship between the paralegals and individual group members.

Practising what you preach

The credibility of the paralegals will depend on their own behaviour. Sonaban was one of those who was a bit over-zealous in the campaign against dowry marriages. She herself has two daughters so all eyes will be on her when they reach marriageable age. The age at which they marry will also be a matter of interest.

Some paralegals have, in their personal lives, benefited by their training. Sajeda, for instance, is one of three sisters whose brother is not giving them their share of their father's property. He has given one sister who is widowed a small fraction of the land, but refuses to give Sajeda or the other sister anything. When Sajeda pointed out to him that between the three sisters they were collectively entitled to three-fifths of the entire property he offered them a small amount each, but Sajeda knows that there is more land and is now trying to get the records from the settlement office so that she can call a *salish*.

Others, however, have problems. For example, Munshi has only one daughter, who is not very pretty, and there will be problems in getting her married. He feels he is unlikely to get her married unless he is willing to pay. So far he has resisted the temptation to offer a dowry to a potential son-in-law, but the social pressures on him to get his daughter married are very great.

It is only when test cases like this and others are won and seen to be won, that the paralegal training programme will be held to have succeeded.

ECONOMISTS IN ECUADOR AND NEPAL — THE BAREFOOT APPROACH TO RURAL DEVELOPMENT PLANNING
Andrew Scott

'A participatory approach means bringing people into not only decision-making but also resource mobilization and management.'

Definition of barefoot economist

In the developed world the expression 'barefoot economist' is finding popularity amongst those with a liking for pithy phrases to describe proponents of the so-called 'new economics'. These economists are highly educated professionals who have either renounced their orthodox training in the world of neo-classical, Keynesian and post-Keynesian economic theory (or who never fully accepted it in the first place.) This kind of 'barefoot economist' believes that 'economics as traditionally professed is too mechanistic to be of any use in the evaluation and interpretation of the problems that affect peasant communities living largely at subsistence levels'. Conventional economics is preoccupied with quantification, and anything not readily measurable is omitted from the economic calculus. A 'barefoot economist', however, is one concerned with the unquantifiable and the economically invisible.

This type of economist also believes in local action and in small dimensions, believing that it is only in such environments that human creativity and meaningful identities can truly surface and flourish. In the 'new economics' the social and economic relations between people are, or should be, of interdependence not of competition and conflict. Similarly, the relationship between people and their physical environment should be non-destructive. As Max-Neef says 'People must, both collectively and individually, feel themselves directly responsible for the consequence of their actions within their environment and this can only happen if the dimension of that environment remains within the human scale.'

In the developing world the adjective 'barefoot' has other connotations of course, which have been earned through particular usage. Suggesting both poverty and mobility, it has been used for a number of years to denote a paraprofessional field worker, someone who is not a full professional or technical expert but who performs the tasks of an expert in the field. 'Paraprofessionals offer a means of providing needed services at low cost to under-serviced publics' (Max-Neef).

The first of these two meanings appears to be used only in the developed world and is associated only with economists, since doctors, lawyers and other professionals of unorthodox or alternative views are not usually described as 'barefoot'. On the other hand, the second usage, while common in development literature, is not normally used in association with economists. So what is a 'barefoot' or paraprofessional economist?

In this paper, drawing upon the published account by a self-proclaimed 'barefoot economist' of the first kind, Manfred Max-Neef, and on accounts of paraprofessional field workers, an attempt is made to illustrate and draw parallels between the two concepts of 'barefoot' and to clarify the term as applied to economists.

Experts in Ecuador

In 1971 the Mision Andina del Ecuador, a government agency, initiated a project for the 'planning of zonal programmes for the modernization of rural life in the Andes'. This was a UNDP-funded project formulated by international experts which concentrated on the planning of rural development in previously neglected areas. Its implementation called for the services of nine UN experts in addition to a Project Manager, Manfred Max-Neef, who relates the story of the project in his book *From the Outside Looking In.*

The project, which went under the name 'ECU-28', was to be a regional planning exercise with the objective of speeding up the development of rural communities. One area was to be selected for which an integrated development programme would be prepared as a model for other areas. Improved methods of programme implementation and of resource allocation were to be formulated and established, and specific projects designed. In short, ECU-28 was to be like many other grand integrated rural development programmes in other parts of the world and was to be under the direction of a professional economist.

However, unlike many integrated area planning projects of the time, ECU-28 specified that the project 'should promote measures to ensure a more active participation of the rural population and facilitate a better utilization of the actual and potential resources'. Max-Neef, a 'barefoot economist' of the first kind, with definite views, interpreted this as a mandate to mobilize the peasants of the selected area, giving them the opportunity to design their own development plan.

Participation, however, can mean many and different things to different people. It has been conceived of in ways which range from people being almost passive recipients of development assistance, to people being fully involved in the decision-making process and in the formulation and implementation of programmes; from people being subjects of development programmes to being initiators. It was clearly the latter end of this spectrum which Max-Neef understood.

The project's experts held two differing views on how the desired participation should be achieved. Some felt that only through 'conscientization' of the people would a necessary change in attitudes be brought about which would enable participation to take place. The others, including Max-Neef, believed that a change in the 'structural inter-relationships' of people and communities was required. This change, however, would have to be stimulated by a catalyst from outside. The question was how and by whom.

The project decided that the required disruption should be stimulated from amongst the peasants themselves, and not by the introduction of 'agents' from outside, whose perceptions would be different from those of the local people. Rather than recruit 'agents' from within the communities to provide the catalytic effect, the catalyst for change would be a process of 'horizontal confrontation and awareness' initiated by the project: 'it seemed plausible to assume that if horizontal links of communication were established and problems reciprocally analysed, interpreted and compared, the 'disruption effort' might come about without the risk of perceptive distortions'. In other words, the change which would enable participation by the people in the target area would be brought about through stimulating changes in the 'structural inter-relationships' between them.

The area for the pilot planning exercise, selected following several months of study by the experts, was in the north-west of Ecuador. Geographically, the area comprises the catchment basin of three rivers, Mira, Cayapas and Santiago, which to some extent is isolated physically from the rest of the country. Covering a total area of 16,600 square kilometres, the region had a population of 357,000 organized into 95 parishes in the provinces of Carchi, Imbabura and Esmeraldas.

After selecting the area for the pilot, the project's experts undertook a reconnaissance of the region to identify the major issues facing the region and devise a strategy for the preparation of a development plan. For this reconnaissance they were able to count on the help and assistance of some of the Mision Anderia del Ecuador (MAE) field workers. The experts concluded that 'A coherent Regional Development Plan must result from the direct participation of grass-roots groups, using expert asssistance only when required'. The horizontal communication between communities which the experts had resolved upon was to be brought about by the establishment in each parish of a Committee of Communication, Information and Relations (CCIR). Each committee should be made up of people representing the local administrative authorities, educators, artisans, small business owners and peasant agriculturalists. The functions of the committees would be to establish contact with other communities in order to generate awareness of their common problems and to serve as permanent points of contact between the project staff and the parish.

Over a period of two months at the end of 1972 a total of 54 CCIRs were established by the experts visiting each community. The experts had also instructed the members of each committee as to what was expected of them. The newly formed committees were then asked to prepare reports on living conditions and problems in their communities, in sections covering education, health, communications, problems of artisans, problems of small landowners and problems of landless peasants. The reports were to be read and discussed and approved by community assemblies.

The diagnostic report from each and every CCIR was received by the Project Staff in Quito, where a synthesis was prepared which constituted a diagnosis of the problems faced by the people of the selected area. This diagnosis was sent to the CCIRs for comment and it was hoped that by reading the document in communal assemblies the rural inhabitants would take their first step towards the formation of a regional consciousness. The revised document was to be the focus for the next stage of the planning process, 'Peasants' Encounters', to be held in Quito.

Three Peasants' Encounters or Meetings were held, one for each of the three provinces, attended by a total of 300 representatives from the CCIRs. Each group met for two days, with the encounters being divided into 'commissions' for health, education, etc. The project experts were there as advisers and assisted as rapporteurs. The outcome was 'a package of admirably coherent projects and proposals', identified and formulated by the communities' representatives. Eighteen specialized reports had been produced, each comprising a description and diagnosis of problems, and an appraisal of previous attempts to tackle them. The reports divided the area into zones of priority, specified the inputs expected to be generated locally and the essential external inputs required, especially financial and technical assistance.

The final stage of the plan preparation exercise was a 'Regional Peasants' Congress', with representatives from every CCIR in the selected region. This Congress agreed that the pilot region should be divided into 12 zones, and that for each zone a development sub-plan would be formulated. It was understood that all the parishes in a zone were to act together in the execution of the different projects in accordance with the priorities of the sub-plan. All the individual projects proposed by the Encounter Commissions were discussed by the Congress. The Congress elected 15 members to a new Regional Planning Commission which would be in charge of the final version of the Regional Rural Development Plan. As a permanent body it would act as a link between the national authorities and CCIRs of the region and would supervise the execution of the many separate projects.

Phase I of the project had ended. Phase II — implementation — never started. During the project the government of Ecuador changed and an authoritarian military dictatorship took over. Any democratic element in the project, and the interpretation of 'participation' taken by the team was highly democratic, was liable to be at risk from the new authorities. The Regional Planning Commission was a democratic body additional to and separate from the established administrative institutions and its existence could threaten the power of the military or at least provide a focus for democratic and opposition forces.

The pilot planning exercise of ECU-28 may be considered successful to the extent that it achieved the full participation of the people it was intended to benefit in the identification of problems, setting of priorities and design of projects. The 'barefoot economist', as Project Manager, was orchestrating this participation and co-ordinating the work of elected committees. However, the nature of the participation pursued, which was in accordance with Max-Neef's 'barefoot' ideas, did not have the support of the new state authorities. A development planning process is one of political economy, and the political aspect is emphasized when planning involves participation in the sense of empowering people to control the development of their community. Implementation of the development plans drawn up under ECU-28 did not take place because the political power of the state did not wish it, so to that extent the project is less successful.

Organizers in Nepal

Participation in the Small Farmer Development Programme of Nepal (SFDP) is participation in a different sense to that attempted in Ecuador. The SFDP is a combination of institutional credit, effective delivery of inputs and services, and organizational development, aimed at disadvantaged sectors of the Nepalese rural population. It motivates small farmers, landless rural workers, fishermen and artisans to form organizations or groups of their own around an income-generating activity, based on group plans and group action, supported by credit and supervised by extension staff.

The SFDP was initiated in 1975 at Mahendranagar in Dhanush District in the Terai. This, and another pilot project in Nuwakot District, were to be action-research projects to determine whether groups of 'small farmers' would be an effective mechanism for the conduct of various social and economic activities for improving welfare and delivery of inputs and services. The project at Mahendranagar was judged a success, with the formation of 32 groups in the first year and 13 in the second. By the end of 1984 a total of 110 groups had been formed under the project there.

SFDP project sites, of which there are now over 250, are selected on the basis of an area survey and the recommendation of the District Sub-project Implementation Committee (SPIC). The area survey, undertaken by government officials, provides information on the topography, climate, land-use pattern, availability of natural resources, farm family structure, incomes and composition of the different ethnic groups in the area. The SPIC is the co-ordinating body at District level for the SFDP, with representatives of the various line agencies. In other words the sites are carefully selected and investigated by the government agencies first. The people of the area do not participate in this exercise except as subjects of study.

Before any activity under the SFDP takes place, the small farmers are organized into groups. The incentive for them to form these groups is the chance to gain access to credit from the

Agricultural Development Bank (ADB) and services from the various line agencies of government. The groups are intended to be the means for small farmers to receive these inputs. The group members (usually 15-20 at most) are required to accept joint liability, though activities undertaken may be on an individual or joint basis. The emphasis is on joint activities and efforts are made to form groups whose members share common interests or characteristics. The groups are organized by an external agent, the Group Organizer (GO) and, as in Ecuador, do not emerge through the initiatives of the small farmers themselves.

A secondary objective of the SFDP is 'to make the small farmers self-reliant in planning and implementation of the development programmes of small farmers'. As the groups become more self-reliant and independent from the GOs and gain more experience and confidence in their development activities, in the longer term the SFDP might lead to the small farmers attempting to transform their environment by collective effort. The horizontal links between groups established through the 'Inter-group Co-ordination Committee' could reinforce this in the way horizontal communication in ECU-28 intended.

The GOs and Women's Group Organizers (WGOs), employees of the Agricultural Development Bank of Nepal, are central to the implementation of the SFDP. They assist the small farmers in the project area to form their groups, to conduct group meetings and keep records and accounts of group activities. Each also works as a motivator, extension worker, and banker, and helps the farmers' groups establish good relations with the several different line agencies involved in the Programme.

On establishment of the SFDP in an area the GO or WGO conducts a detailed household survey covering such factors as income, labour use, consumption pattern, skills, land use, literacy, health and nutritional status. This helps him or her to identify the small farmers in the area with whom (s)he should work. The main task of the GO is then to form groups of these small farmers to take advantage of the SFDP. The groups are generally formed around some specific income-generating project. The support provided by the GO is not intended to be permanent and when the groups have reached a stage where they can function independently, the GO withdraws.

At Kumroj, for example, where the SFDP was introduced in 1980, the question of irrigation was raised by the villagers. The GO met a number of villagers and discussed their previous experiences in using the local river for irrigation. Villagers at the river's source had not been able to irrigate their land, and were antagonistic towards any efforts to construct a canal to irrigate fields several kilometres away. Rich villagers at the source, who had been exploiting others, feared losing their power. The villagers also needed financial and technical help to construct the canal, which was not available to them prior to the introduction of SFDP in the area. Having determined the situation in the village, the GO assisted the farmers at the river's source to design an irrigation project which they could implement. The farmers formed a canal construction committee and started work with technical assistance from the SFDP. Representatives were selected to form committees for construction, land-use compensation, labour mobilization, water management and distribution, water rent collection and milling and marketing.

The GO at Kumroj was successful in organizing the farmers and motivating them for participation in the project. The success of this small project encouraged others to undertake their own projects.

The GOs have varied functions for which they receive three months' pre-service training at the Agricultural Credit Training Institute. This training amounts to orientation of the participants towards the aims and objectives of the SFDP and the procedures to be followed in its implementation. The training course also briefs them about various development programmes and about ways of improving the socio-economic position of small farmers. In-service training is also provided periodically at the ACTI. The training approach is intended to be practical, with up to half the time spent in the field on existing projects.

The GOs and WGOs of the Agricultural Development Bank are paraprofessionals, carrying out tasks which in other programmes and societies would be performed by economists. Household surveys, identification of target groups, project identification and formulation are undertaken either working alone or in conjunction with the groups they have helped establish. Though linked with a credit delivery system, their purpose and that of the SFDP is more than the provision and effective delivery of credit to the poor. They can be regarded as 'barefoot economists'.

'Barefoot economists' of this kind are not unique to Nepal, though they have not been called this and their work is not well documented. There is, however, no single model for a 'barefoot economist': the details of their organizations and duties vary from place to place. In Bolivia, for example, the National Community Development Service, established in 1964, relies on paraprofessionals to assist communities to gain access to health and agricultural services. The *promotores* are mostly men with little formal education and they come from the communities they serve. They are responsible for finding solutions to problems and for assisting community leaders in project planning, budgeting and implementation. They also supervise initiation of subsequent projects. In Sri Lanka, the paraprofessional with this role has been called a 'change agent'. There the paraprofessional's role is to break the structural barriers (as in ECU-28) which prevent villagers taking charge of their own lives.

Conclusions

The concept of a 'barefoot economist' in the developed world and the paraprofessional concept in the developing world, emphasize the facilitation of people's participation in the development of their own communities — and participation which is more than that of a subject or accepter of development activities. The 'barefoot economist' is in both cases part of a system intended to bring about this participation. Max-Neef, as a professional economist with 'barefoot' ideas, was at the head of such an organization. The Group Organizers of the ADBN on the other hand are the troops of their organization, near the bottom of the hierarchy. In the latter case the economist's functions are more decentralized, with the paraprofessionals undertaking surveys and analysis away from the professionals.

Oakley and Marsden have identified two different practices of the role of the 'agent of participation': to facilitate the access of the group to resources for development (as in Nepal); and to develop awareness within the group and build up the strength and the organizational base of groups of rural poor (as in ECU-28). The paraprofessional economist is primarily of the first type (sometimes with various aspects of the second) and is akin to the more well-known and near-ubiquitous Community Development worker.

Max-Neef describes outside experts in development programmes who 'instead of acting as they should, that is, as "catalysts" for the development of hidden potential, act as they should not, that is, as "doers" of things that are often not desired.' For paraprofessionals too, the role of catalyst is central. There is nothing new in economists' work being undertaken by paraprofessionals: the phrase 'barefoot economist' can usefully emphasize this role, and direct training needs to strengthen this important aspect of their work.

BANKERS IN BANGLADESH — GIVING CREDIT WHERE CREDIT IS DUE
Ken Marshall

One of the most enthusiastic women at the inauguration of the Grameen Bank by Bangladesh's Finance Minister was Zamiran, a member of one of several loan groups established in Jamurki village, some 60 miles north of the capital city, Dhaka. Zamiran is the wife of a landless labourer, Amzad Ali, who could only find casual seasonal labour to maintain a family of four children. She described it as a 'one meal a day' family in 1980 — a clear indication of its poor socio-economic status. They owned no agricultural land, lived in a *kutcha* straw hut and had no animals. By 1985, by dint of five Grameen Bank loans, hard work and enterprise, Zamiran transformed the family into a three meal a day family, able to mortgage in 25 decimals (0.25 acres) of agricultural land, living in a house protected by a *pucca* tin roof, owning five pieces of furniture, four animals and more than a dozen poultry birds.

This dramatic transformation was occasioned by her taking a series of small loans (all paid off on time), undertaking multiple occupations and reinvesting profits. The loans were made by Grameen Bank. The first loan was paid off quickly — within six months of the twelve-month loan period — with the profits from the paddy husking sufficient to pay the total loan amount plus interest and the profits from cow fattening used to pay for a tin roof for the house. The second loan was repaid with profits from milk and eggs from the livestock and poultry, and the additional profits from milk sales and eventual sale of the cow were used to mortgage in 25 decimals of land for farming by Zamiran's husband and only son, a further source of income to the family.

Since these two significantly productive loans, Zamiran has continued to take and quickly repay what have effectively become working-capital loans, which have enabled her to expand the scale of her paddy husking business and diversify into goat rearing, as well as continuing to alternate between the seasonal activities of milch cow rearing and cattle fattening.

Table 2: Loan record of Zamiran

Loan	Repayment (months)	Amount (Taka)	Amount (US$)	Purpose
1	6	1,000	30	cow fattening (600) paddy husking (400)
2	4	2,000	60	milch cow (1,900) chickens (60) ducks (40)
3	8	2,000	60	cow fattening (800) paddy husking (1,200)
4	8	1,000	30	goat rearing (500) paddy husking (500)
5	6	4,000	120	milch cow (2,200) housing (1,800)

Each loan has been invested in a mix of activities dictated by Zamiran's knowledge of local market opportunities, with one activity used to pay back the full loan amount and the other activities used to meet expanded consumption needs and investments in housing improvements and additional animals. Zamiran's enterprise was underwritten by loans from an innovative credit programme, the Grameen Bank, specially designed and implemented for the landless of Bangladesh.

The Grameen Bank

In July 1979, Bangladesh Bank, the country's central bank, launched the Grameen Bank project, an experimental credit programme to provide unsecured loans to landless households, defined as those owning less than 0.5 acres of agricultural land or assets of equivalent value. The programme was designed to extend loans to enable the landless to undertake a range of income-generating activities such as rice processing, rickshaw driving, livestock rearing, weaving and trading. The project had developed out of an action-research project designed and directed by an economics professor at the Chittagong University, Dr Muhammad Yunus.

Dr Yunus' initial research had been intended to demonstrate that rural credit programmes in Bangladesh were in reality agricultural credit programmes and as such could not reach the country's growing number of functionally landless households which accounted for almost 50 per cent of the country's 12 million rural households. As a result, 80 per cent of rural credit needs were met by recourse to the informal credit market where loan conditions (including effective interest rates as high as 400 per cent a year) were pauperizing marginal landowning households and transferring control of resources, particularly land, to the money-lending classes. This research included a small experimental project with one bank at Jobra village near the University campus. Loans were made to landless individuals with Dr Yunus himself standing guarantor for each loan as required by banking procedures. There followed several exchanges between Dr Yunus and central and commercial bank officials at credit workshops organized in the late 1970s to discuss issues of rural credit. These provided Yunus with the opportunity to challenge conventional banking wisdom which said that the poor were a bad credit risk and that all credit had to be secured against tangible assets, thereby automatically excluding the very poor. As a result, Dr Yunus was requested in 1979 by the central bank to undertake a larger action-research project.

By early 1981 the Grameen Bank Project had established 25 branches in collaboration with the country's nationalized commercial banks. Given this successful expansion and the maintenance of a loan recovery record of 99 per cent, the Bangladesh Bank agreed to a further round of expansion so that Grameen had 100 branches by 1983. As both phases confirmed the viability and replicability of the concept of giving unsecured credit to poor rural households, a more ambitious plan was drawn up not only to expand further but also to create a separate autonomous bank. After careful planning — particularly of the financial and legal aspects of establishing a new bank — the Grameen Bank was formally constituted as an autonomous financial institution specializing in supplying credit to the landless, in September 1983. By September 1987 the Bank had 347 branches working in about 10 per cent of the country's villages. Currently, it has over 290,000 borrowers — 230,000 women and 60,000 men, an unusually high proportion of female borrowers. Monthly loan disbursements are running at US$1.5 million and on-time loan recovery is 97.3 per cent. In addition, in the past three financial years, the Bank has earned a profit on its lending operation, in defiance of all the conventional banking wisdom previously brought to bear on the subject of rural credit.

Organizing principles

The Bank is essentially organized into village-based branches, each run by a branch manager assisted by up to six bank workers — both male and female — who are responsible for identifying and organizing groups of five borrowers (all-male or all-female) from landless households of the selected villages. At maturity each branch (after 24 to 36 months) typically covers 300-400 groups or 1,500-2,000 borrowers. Group members must not be related and their claims, particularly to being landless, are carefully checked by the bank workers by asking questions of others in the village. To qualify for Grameen Bank membership, the five individual group members are required to undertake a seven-day training programme including regular attendance at daily group meetings and daily savings of one taka per member. After this training period the members undergo a probationary period of several weeks during which they are required to attend regular weekly meetings and make weekly contributions of one taka each to the Group Fund. At the end of this period two of the group members become eligible for loans. Once the first two members have established a regular repayment record, then the next two members become eligible for loans. Groups are federated in village level centres, with loans to both groups and centres liable to be interrupted if any one borrower or group defaults on repayments. The result of this 'peer pressure' system of loan security has been an unusually high recovery rate from households considered by Bangladesh's banking fraternity to be bad credit risks.

The loan system has been characterized by strict attention to rules and discipline and application of commercial standards. Interest was initially charged at 13 per cent, the bank base rate until 1984, and subsequently raised to 16 per cent and recently 18 per cent. Loan repayments are made in equal instalments over a 50-week period with weeks 51 and 52 following the 50-week principal repayment period. Additional programme features include active participation by group members themselves in assessing each others' loan requests and compulsory investment in two savings funds, the Group Fund and the Emergency Fund. Five per cent of each loan taken is deducted from the loan payment and credited to a Group Fund held on account by the Bank for investment activities decided by the group. Thus from a US$100 loan the borrower actually receives US$95 and repays the full US$100, while US$5 is credited to the Group Fund. The Emergency Fund is an additional savings source, calculated at 25 per cent of the interest rate and payable at the same time as the interest.

Borrowers are expected to make overdue repayments either from savings or from future profits on their business. Where an individual borrower is in arrears, the pressure for repayment is exercised through fellow group members and, in some cases, overdues are paid off by the whole group from the Group Fund or from a group-run business. When this happens the recalcitrant group member is occasionally replaced — a decision taken not by the Bank but by the group. Where groups or centres are in arrears, the Bank is able to exercise pressure by slowing down new loan disbursements through a branch.

Staff and training

The staff training programme is a unique blend of classroom instruction and on-the-job training lasting for six months — approximately one month in the lecture hall and five months in the field under the supervision of a branch manager. By the end of 1983 the training unit, operating from rented premises and using in-house and outside resource people, had trained 19 batches of bank workers (400 in number) and ten batches of bank managers (160 in number), sufficient given a drop-out rate of ten per cent to meet the needs of what was by then a 100-branch operation employing 480 staff. Recently, the Bank has increased the size of its training unit to six programme officers and increased training capacity to 600 trainees a year to meet its need for over 3,000 branch workers by 1990, in addition to supervisory staff at area, district and HQ levels.

Male bank worker trainees are university graduates with at least a first degree and are expected to work anywhere in the country. By contrast, given the social restrictions on women, female bank workers are higher secondary school certificate holders expected to work in their home areas. In spite of these constraints, half of all bank workers are female. Training materials have been developed largely in-house from case studies collected by successive groups of trainees. These have been supplemented by use of audio-visual aids.

Monitoring and evaluation

A monitoring and evaluation department (MED) has been one of the many unique features of the Bank. It was especially created to monitor the Bank's performance in reaching the poor and in maintaining its high rate of recovery. MED is responsible for producing a monthly spread sheet containing up-to-date information on lending performance disaggregated by gender and district. The spread sheet is a consolidated summary of 20 separate data sheets which allow management to monitor closely the performance of individual branches, district, loan category, gender and so forth. This timely access to management information (recently transferred onto micro-computers) is an essential feature of a system designed to track the Bank's performance at three levels — termed by the Bank as its management, earnings and loan performances. Use of computers has facilitated the introduction of modern management techniques including performance-to-plan budgeting (a system of measuring performance against annual budgets) and ratio analysis (a system of measuring key indicators such as loans made, recoveries, profits and overdues against each other, over time and comparing trends).

Organization and financing

In its initial phase of experimentation and expansion, Grameen Bank was organized as a project of the Central Bank, and the country's commercial banks, all nationalized concerns, were instructed to collaborate by providing credit to landless groups organized under the project. Grameen Bank workers were recruited and effectively seconded to work at the local branch level of whichever particular bank was designated for a particular area. The branch manager was supposed to provide the loan amount sanctioned by the Grameen team but had no personal loan-sanctioning powers.

However, this did not work out in practice in spite of instructions from the Central Bank. Gradually, as the experiment expanded, the project found the delays caused by unco-operative branch managers an impediment to the smooth operation of the scheme. These delays were not found uniformly across all branches, but reflected local variations. Some banks and some branch managers within one bank were found to be more co-operative than others. An added factor to increasing bank disinterest in further expansion of the scheme was the fact that all local costs of the Grameen teams were met by the participating banks, who claimed that the small interest margin (13 per cent) on the small volume of lending was not sufficient to cover these costs (variously estimated at close to 20 per cent, including the cost of capital at a little over 5 per cent (half provided by the Central Bank at 8 per cent and half by IFAD at 3 per cent)).

As a result, it became clear that any significant expansion of the scheme beyond the 100 branches reached in 1983 would require establishment of a separate banking institution especially created to provide credit to landless households. In a remarkably short time, the decision was taken and implemented to establish the Grameen Bank under the GB Ordinance passed in 1983 by the Ministry of Finance. The Bank was given a 12-member board (including two Grameen borrowers), initial paid-up capital of US$1 million and a wide range of banking functions, including deposit mobilization. The general rules continued to apply in terms of borrower eligibility, loan terms, etc.

As a Central Bank project, Grameen was supported by loans of over US$7 million from the central bank and IFAD to create a revolving loan fund. In addition, IFAD and the Ford Foundation provided grant funds to meet the costs of staff training, work aids, and monitoring and evaluation. The costs of central and zonal administration were met by the central bank, local branch costs were met by the participating banks, partly funded out of the interest spread earned on loans made.

By 1983, the project was achieving widespread publicity because of its 99 per cent recovery from the country's poorer households — in marked contrast to the agricultural banks which were rarely recovering 50 per cent of dues and the industrial banks whose recoveries were below 10 per cent! Donor interest was such that the newly constituted Grameen Bank was able to sell quickly its expansion programme to three major donors, IFAD, NORAD and SIDA, who agreed to provide close to US$40 million to enable the Bank to expand its branch operation from 150 in 1985 to 500 by 1990. These funds have been provided as a loan by IFAD and as grants by NORAD and SIDA to the Bangladesh government who will in turn on-lend the funds to Grameen Bank at 6 per cent repayable over 15 years following a five-year period of grace. According to detailed projections prepared by Grameen and IFAD, the profits on a 500-branch operation lending to as many as 3 to 4 million people and earning an interest spread of 12 per cent will be sufficient — given a continuation of high recovery rates — to pay all the running costs of the Bank (including depreciation) and repay the donor credits within 15 years. Then profits would be available to fund further expansion without recourse to external finance. Currently, in spite of being in the middle of expansion to 500 branches, adding 5-6 new branches every month, the Bank has earned a profit in each of its last three financial years. Given that it takes a branch about two years to reach break-even, the Bank is now in a position where its mature branches are generating sufficient funds to meet the Bank's overhead costs plus losses made by new branches in their first two years. Most significantly, the Bank's head office and its zonal offices lend funds to the branches at 10 per cent, with each branch becoming a separate profit centre with its own budgets and performance targets.

Types of business

In the very participative style adopted by Grameen Bank, borrowers are free to choose the type of business in which they invest. A verbal loan proposal is then made by a prospective borrower at the weekly centre meeting. The borrower then has to convince the other members of his or her group of the viability of the proposed business. In turn the group has to convince the bank worker. A recent bank listing showed over 420 types of business in which members had invested either individually or collectively. These were broadly classified into seven categories — manufacturing, agriculture and forestry, livestock and fisheries, services, trading, peddling and shopkeeping. In the case of male borrowers the most popular activity categories are shopkeeping and trading, which account for 51 per cent of loans, followed by livestock and fisheries (22 per cent) and manufacturing (14 per cent). Female borrowers concentrate mainly on livestock and fisheries (55 per cent) and manufacturing (30 per cent).

The top 25 business types accounted for 83 per cent of lending in 1986, the most popular types for male and female borrowers being listed in the Table.

Table 3: Popular businesses for borrowers

MALE BORROWERS — TOP FIVE BUSINESSES (37% OF LOANS):
Milch cow rearing
Paddy and rice trading
Cattle fattening
Rickshaw pulling
Crop trading

FEMALE BORROWERS — TOP FIVE BUSINESSES (74% OF LOANS):
Milch cow rearing
Paddy husking
Cattle fattening
Goat rearing
Paddy trading

The range of activities open to women can be seen to be particularly narrow, reflecting the constraint on women's mobility arising from the tradition of *purdah* or seclusion. Increasing poverty — particularly among widows — is beginning slowly to break down seclusion, however. As this happens women are able to undertake a wider range of activities, especially if these are organized collectively with a group of women investing as partners in a business. Women have thus been able to invest in crop production by leasing in land or in agroprocessing industries by setting up rice-mills. Grameen Bank has also created a technical resource unit within the Bank to investigate and promote new and improved businesses. This is helping women's centres to invest in new businesses such as beekeeping and mechanical rice-milling, and male centres to invest in power tillers and aquaculture.

Impact

A major evaluation by the Bangladesh Institute of Development Studies was designed to assess the Bank's effectiveness in reaching its client group, its loan recovery record, the incremental income flows to borrowers, their incremental expenditure patterns and the cost of credit delivery. The study concluded that, unlike non-borrower households, borrowers had achieved significant real income gains, typically 30 per cent over the two-year period studied, in contrast to the stagnant real income performance of non-GBP households. These income gains were used for both investment and consumption purposes and resulted, among other things, in increased expenditure on health, education and housing, particularly in the case of female borrowers.

Credit has proved to be an extremely effective entry point for Grameen Bank in working with Bangladesh's rural poor. Its excellent results to date stand in marked contrast to the more complex, multi-functional area development programmes which have tried to work simultaneously across several sectors and issues — credit, skill training, technology, health, education, etc. The Bank's programme has been designed to meet members' most immediate needs — in this case, for credit readily available in small amounts and easily accessible. Gradually, as the organization's strength has built up, so additional components have been added.

Through the contacts made by both Group and Centre leaders as well as bank workers, members have been able to arrange immunization for themselves and their children, installation of hand tubewells for drinking water supply, vaccination for their cattle and poultry and other sevices previously only notionally available to them. They have been able to improve access to these services not only because of improved purchasing power but also because of the strength of their organization. Credit from the Grameen Bank has proved to be only the first step in a process of empowerment which has begun to reduce the dependency of landless members on the monopolistic elements — particularly moneylenders and traders — who dominate rural life in Bangladesh. With small but timely amounts of credit, individuals have been able to build up that element of financial security necessary to longer-term survival. In addition, as group cohesion and strength have grown, the landless have been able to participate in village politics, contesting election to local public office and using group strength to bid for lucrative leases on government-owned resources such as market places, fishponds, forest land and roadside verges.

Following workshops organized by the Bank for centre leaders, the members have instituted a set of principles of conduct and social action collectively known as the Sixteen Decisions. Included are the pledges:
○ we will arrange schooling for our children
○ we will grow more vegetables
○ we will improve our houses
○ we will drink tubewell water
○ we will not give or accept dowry
○ we will maintain loan discipline
○ we will work collectively as groups and centres.

Conclusion

The Grameen Bank has directly helped to raise the incomes of the poor, mobilized savings and put under-employed resources and people to productive work. Indirectly — and as importantly — it has improved the bargaining power of the poor by increasing their options for credit and work. Finally, it has raised the confidence of the rural poor in themselves, created collective strength and improved the socio-economic status of women. This process of development and change has already been brought to 5 per cent of the villages and landless households of rural Bangladesh.

Grameen Bank has been able to provide credit at rates of interest which encourage productive economic activity and cover the costs of fund mobilization and loan administration. One of the key features of the system has been careful credit supervision by bank workers which has enabled the Bank to maintain unusually high rates of credit recovery, which in turn make the relatively high staff to borrower ratios profitable and are enabling the Bank to continue its expansion programme.

Similar, albeit smaller, programmes in Bangladesh and neighbouring India are strong testimony to the success of this formula when underwritten by dedicated management and motivated staff, in this case all Bangladeshi, and careful problem identification and action research to design and develop working systems. An essential element in the Bank's success has been its ability to learn lessons and adapt its systems. The unprecedented floods of 1987 brought pressure for rescheduling of part of the Bank's loan portfolio and the Bank is currently considering its response which may require some modification to its procedures.

Finally, by showing that the poor are a sound credit risk, Grameen Bank has pointed the way to a new system of credit provision and human development in which people gain control over their own lives through economic self-reliance and collective action. However, the success of institutions like Grameen Bank suggests that the existing banking system is inadequate to the task of poverty alleviation. What is needed are new banking structures with largely generalist staff taking credit to the people in the villages.

MANAGEMENT CONSULTANTS IN KENYA — THE PROVISION OF BAREFOOT BUSINESS SERVICES

Malcolm Harper

The millions of small business and 'informal sector' operators in developing countries are themselves perhaps the most numerous and powerful example of the 'barefoot' approach to the provision of services. Without the benefit of external encouragement or funding, and motivated only by their own need to survive, these people create jobs for themselves, their families and employees and also provide a whole host of goods and services at prices and in places which are convenient for the poor.

There are numerous attempts to provide assistance of various sorts such as credit, training and advice to small enterprises. Many of these have failed because they have been delivered by highly qualified staff, who need expensive buildings to work from and expensive vehicles to travel in. They have failed not only because the delivery costs are so high in relation to the very small proportion of small enterprises they can reach, but also because their staff are often remote from the real world of the people they are trying to help, even to the extent of not knowing the language. After all, people struggle for an education in order to leave behind the squalid world of informal enterprise. They are unlikely to be willing to re-enter that world as advisers, bankers or trainers and, if they do, they are unlikely to have the right knowledge or attitudes to do an effective job.

A number of agencies, both local and international, official and voluntary, have appreciated this problem and have decided to learn something from the clients whom they are trying to help. Can their assistance not be delivered by the same modest methods and ordinary people used by their clients, cannot barefoot businesses be served by barefoot bankers, barefoot consultants or barefoot trainers?

It could be argued that these barefoot entrepreneurs have little need of external assistance; all they need is to be allowed to get on with their work. Many of them demonstrate a truly amazing degree of enterprise, tenacity, flexibility, hard work and physical courage in starting and maintaining their businesses in the face of unrestricted competition and total neglect or often sheer hostility on the part of governments. Their products or services may not be of the highest 'quality', but they are nevertheless appropriate for the available resources and markets they serve. Their producers display amazing local skills in making use of a whole range of discarded materials. There is little that a qualified engineer can offer in the way of advice to the average village blacksmith or roadside mechanic and a chartered accountant would be unlikely to be of much use to a market shopkeeper or itinerant hawker. Most of these business people are forced by circumstances to make optimum use of their limited capital and to respond to the needs of the market place. They lack the protection of government or of private monopoly, and must be efficient to survive.

Some of these people, particularly those who are attempting to make the transition from informal to formal status, can nevertheless benefit from external advice. They need help to bridge the gap between themselves and the official world with which they must communicate if they are to progress beyond a certain size. They need help to prepare loan applications, to obtain licences, to select, acquire, install and operate new equipment, to use new materials, to acquire materials which are only available from formal sources, to find premises and to make use of more 'modern' means of promotion. All these require information and, particularly, contacts which are usually outside the world of the traditional small-scale business person. There is, therefore, a role for external advice, but, for the reasons already suggested, traditional business and technical consultants are too expensive, too scarce, and in general 'inappropriate' for this task. Might this not be an opportunity for a barefoot approach?

A case study from Kenya

An experiment was undertaken in the early 1970s in Kenya to develop and test such an approach, employing fourth form school leavers who had failed to proceed to the fifth and sixth years of secondary school, with no business experience, to provide appropriate management consultancy to rural shopkeepers. The young consultants (this term was used deliberately to enhance their self-respect and to compensate, in part at least, for the salary of $20 a month which was all that a university research budget would allow) were selected from vast numbers of applicants who presented themselves in the two districts where the experiment was to be carried out. The ensuing mob was first of all told about the job, and was warned of the salary, the temporary nature of the job and the lack of any travel allowances or transport facilities. This reduced them to a more manageable number and they were then given a very brief written test to gauge their ability to carry out simple arithmetical calculations and to appreciate some of the most basic aspects of business. They were also asked to prepare a simple sketch map of their home region in order to observe their written presentation skills and to find out where they lived and what businesses were in the area, since they were to work from home and had to be within walking distance of a reasonable number of markets. Those who passed this test were interviwed for a few minutes, to judge their initiative and their ability to respond to unexpected questions.

Six people were selected from each of the two regions, and were trained for two months; as a final selection device, they were warned that only four of them would actually be employed as consultants; the two weakest in each region would have to leave after training.

The training itself consisted of two days a week of classroom sessions; they spent the other days attached to local shops and other businesses, who agreed to take them as free labour in return for answering their questions. They completed simple assignments in each business, involving basic diagnosis of business practices, and also worked on exercises on financial management and diagnosis, and recommendations for improved management in such areas as stock selection and control, promotion and simple record keeping.

After a final test, which was mainly a pretext for the dismissal of the two who had not shown the necessary ability, although they had clearly identified themselves earlier, the consultants were sent into the field. Because the periods of business attachment during the training had progressed from observation through diagnosis to recommenadtion, the transition from training to consultancy was in a sense gradual; when they were in the field, they had fortnightly half-day sessions when they shared their clients' problems with one another, presenting them very much in the same way as they had learned during the training exercises.

The consultants advised a total of around 200 shops; the impact of their advice was measured after six months through simple before-and-after observation, and by asking the clients at the end of the period whether they would be willing to pay $1 for each visit in future. Although the service had been free up to that time, about 70 per cent of the clients said that they would be willing to pay; they felt that their improved results would justify such a charge.

The experiment was then concluded, although one or two of the consultants were encouraged by the positive reaction of their clients to continue with the work, without the benefit of the very close supervision they had had during the experiment, and for a fee. The others, as well as those who had been dropped after the training, succeeded in finding jobs although they had all previously been unemployed. This was a rewarding by-product of the experiment.

This Kenyan experiment has been described in some detail, partly because it was closely monitored and evaluated. It was nevertheless very limited: the clients were only advised for six months, only shopkeepers were included, in the interests of homogeneity and ease of testing and evaluation; and the short duration and lack of any institutional base prevented the development of relationships with banks and other sources of small business services which are such an essential part of programmes of this type.

Experiences elsewhere

Similar 'barefoot' business consulting services have subsequently been provided in a number of different places, sharing some aspects of the Kenyan experiment but based mainly on local circumstances. Table 4 summarizes, briefly, some aspects of eight of these programmes. The information may in some cases be out of date, as such services evolve, change and may indeed cease to operate at all in response to circumstances, but the Table does illustrate the diversity of possibilities.

Degree of 'barefootedness'

The degree of 'barefootedness' depends on local circumstances and, in particular, on the relationship between the employment situation and the output of the various levels of education. It has generally been found appropriate to recruit consultants from the highest level of education at which a substantial number of people still fail to find employment. Since educational output is almost always ahead of employment opportunites, this ensures that the consultants are above average in intelligence and persistence, since they have achieved a higher than average level of education. They are, nevertheless, 'hungry'; they are unlikely to be alienated from their home environment by their education

Table 4: Experiences in barefoot business consultancy services

LOCATION	AGENCY	SERVICE	QUALIFICATIONS	BUSINESS	FUNDING
Cali, Colombia	DESAP Program of Fundacion Carvajal	Consultancy integrated	junior university	manufacturing	client fees + Foundation
Bhaktapur, Nepal	Industrial Promotion Centre GTZ Project	Consultancy	secondary school	manufacturing	German aid
Botswana	Partnership for Productivity (PfP) Botswana	Consultancy	junior secondary school	trading	foreign donors
Kenya	PfP Kenya	Consultancy	secondary school	all types	foreign donors + client fees
Malawi	Development of Malawian Traders	Consultancy	secondary school	trading, later manufacturing	foreign donors + client fees
Kaolack, Senegal	Community & Enterprise Assistance	Loans + consultancy	secondary school	agricultural related enterprises	foreign donors to be replaced by earnings from loan scheme
Hargeisa, Somalia (refugee camps)	PfP Somalia	Consultancy + technical training	secondary school	manufacturing	foreign donors
Port Sudan	EuroAction Acord	Consultancy + loans	secondary school	manufacturing	fees, interest earnings + donors

and they recognize that comfortable, white-collar capital city employment is unlikely to be within their reach. They are therefore willing to work in rural areas and urban shanty towns, and accept the modest salaries which are necessary if such services are to be economic.

Transport is a vexed problem in most developing countries; access to a vehicle is an important source of status, a valuable resource and a frequent cause of friction. Vehicles, with their maintenance and fuel costs are expensive to run, particularly in relation to local incomes. None of the business advisers in these services has a car at his or her disposal. Some have bicycles, some have motorcycles and others walk or use public transport. This may be the single most obvious distinction between them and other advisers.

Nature of training

The original Kenyan experiment was undertaken in the field because it was realized that classroom training was of little value to most small-scale business people, since they were unable to be away from their businesses for any significant amount of time and their limited education made it difficult for them to adjust to a classroom situation (especially if their competitors were present) and to apply to their own businesses what they had learned in general terms. There are, however, services such as the DESAP programme in Cali, Colombia, where a formal course of classroom training is effectively integrated with one-to-one field consultancy to assist in the implementation of what has been learned. In other cases, classroom training is provided by the consultants or others on an *ad hoc* basis when it appears that a number of clients need to know the same thing. Technical training can also be provided in conjunction with this type of consultancy, as is being done for refugees in Somalia. Trainees can be assisted on site to start or expand their businesses once they have received the technical training which will enable them to do this.

Combining technical and business advice

In some places, attempts are being made to combine technical and business advice. This is obviously desirable, if it proves to be possible, since in the vast majority of small enterprises the management function is not separated from the technical one. The same person is responsible for both, and a consultant who only addresses management problems is perceived by most business people as being concerned with what is by far the least important of the two functions. It is hoped that in the future an approach can be evolved whereby barefoot consultants can be trained to offer a 'value engineering' service to all types of small-scale manufacturing enterprises, by asking the right questions about materials, processes and so on. At this stage, the best that can be achieved is a referral system, whereby the generalist barefoot consultant has been trained to recognize situations where technical expertise is necessary, which may then be made available by specialists within their organizations or elsewhere. There are usually insufficient businesses of only one type in any one area to justify specialist barefoot technology consultants, but this remains an area for future experimentation.

The question of credit

Opinions differ as to whether loans should or should not be provided by the same service which employs the consultant. On the one hand, a consultant without lending responsibilities will be perceived as a source of advice, rather than cash, and will therefore be more likely to obtain frank information on which to base his diagnosis and recommendation. If the client has borrowed money, a consultant who is also responsible for the loan will be perceived as a debt collector rather than an adviser; this also pollutes consultant/client relationships. On the other hand, although unthinking loan hunger or the capital shortage illusion are all too prevalent, there is a genuine need for finance, and advisers without access to it may be regarded as irrelevant. In addition, lending may be the only way in which consultants can eventually pay their way. Fees can be and are charged in some places, but are usually no more than a small proportion of the total costs. Higher than average interest rates are of little significance to small-scale borrowers, but can make a significant contribution to the cost of a consultancy service.

Self-financing services

It could be argued that such self-sustainability can only be achieved if the barefoot advisers become little more than barefoot moneylenders, who are already all too familiar as providers of allegedly extortionate credit to small-scale farmers and others. However, experience with formal credit schemes has frequently shown that moneylenders actually provide a better service, even though their interest rates are several times higher, because of their rapid service and the lack of expensive, intimidating and time-consuming formalities. Extortion undoubtedly occurs, but barefoot banking can itself be a viable enterprise and can be combined with barefoot consultancy of the sort described.

There are a number of examples of this type of operation, particularly in the Philippines. Manila Community Services Inc (MSCI), for instance, has enormously increased the outreach of its market trader credit programme by setting up its initial borrowers, who are themselves market women, as retailers of a credit which MSCI now only wholesales. The spread earned by these women enables them to offer an effective service whereby they not only extend credit but also offer friendly advice to large numbers of their less experienced fellow traders. They themselves are increasing their income, credit and advice are made available to more people, and MSCI have secured a delivery system which is far less expensive and more effective than employing its own staff.

Any agency providing externally supported services for enterprises should aim to 'put itself out of business', either by developing its clients to the level at which they have no further need of its services or, more realistically since the numbers are so large and new entrants are continually coming up, by helping barefoot bankers, advisers, trainers and others to become self-supporting enterprises themselves. Those who are better shod are too expensive, too few and too disqualified by their fortune to provide much in the way of useful services to small enterprises. The barefoot approach can eventually lead to employment opportunities and improved services for small business, from which external assistance can be withdrawn with confidence.

VILLAGE ARTISANS IN BOTSWANA — THE TRAINING OF BAREFOOT TECHNICIANS
David Inger

There has been growing recognition in recent years that whilst the potential for job creation in the 'modern', usually capital-intensive sector, is severely limited, there is often considerable potential for expanding the 'informal' sector. The informal sector is variously defined, but usually includes people who work part-time at a fairly low level of production, are largely self-employed, have little in the way of business premises or equipment and are outside the framework of business regulations, licensing and tax. Tinsmiths, carpenters, cobblers and 'bush mechanics' are typical examples.

However, the countries with the most flourishing informal sector have tended to be ones with a relatively large, or concentrated, population and a lack of access to cheap mass-produced goods, often coupled with problems such as lack of foreign exchange.

Botswana's economic environment displays none of these features, and at first sight is not likely to be conducive to informal sector development. With a population of one million spread over an area considerably larger than France, there is a limited potential market. Botswana is also heavily dependent on South Africa and is a member of the Southern African Customs Union. There is no provision within this agreement for protecting small-scale industries and Botswana is thus dominated by centralized mass-production industries, either in South Africa or in the urban enclave within Botswana. Botswana also displays many of the symptoms of a classic dual economy. With two of the largest diamond mines in the world and 14 months of foreign exchange reserves, it has one of the highest per capita average incomes in the developing world. However, more than half of the population live below the 'poverty datum line', a statistical concept which defines only the most basic human needs in terms of nutrition, shelter and clothing and 60 per cent of the population are currently receiving government emergency food rations after five years of drought.

The village artisan training programme

It was against this unpromising background that the Rural Industries Innovation Centre (RIIC) decided to embark on its Village Artisan Training Programme in 1980. The goal was to try and create an increasing number of 'barefoot technicians' who would work within the informal sector, using local materials and locally produced tools as much as possible to provide a variety of support services to other producers, especially farmers. It was believed that although it is almost impossible to compete with mass-produced goods and services on the small- and medium-scale, it might be possible for these barefoot technicians and producers to succeed at the 'micro-scale'. They would have no overheads and would require a minimal amount of working capital. Some of them would come from fairly remote settlements with limited access to the mass-produced goods distribution system and low incomes. Nevertheless there would still be some basic needs related to the technician's skills, whether it be producing a coffin or repairing a plough.

The village tannery unit

The first project to be started, in 1980, was the village tannery unit. Botswana has over two million cattle, thousands of sheep and goats and perhaps one of the largest national wildlife herds in the world. Unlike other countries', this wildlife resource is considerably under-utilized. Botswana has a policy of conservation combined with controlled exploitation of wildlife for those species which are over-stocked. The ownership of cattle is very unevenly distributed, with half of the national cattle herd being owned by seven per cent of the households. When it comes to wildlife however, many of the poorest people still rely on hunting and gathering for survival. For this group in particular, skins have tended not to be regarded as a useful by-product.

In order to maintain the philosophy of maximizing the use of local materials, some research was necessary to assess the tannin content of local trees, shrubs and roots. A number of satisfactory sources were found, but more recently it was discovered that *jatropha terminalia* is highly effective and can reduce the time necessary for tanning by almost half.

The tannery offers training both at the RIIC itself and in the field.

A typical field project is the one undertaken in 1980 in the Kweneng District, in the western desert area. A local development trust in one of the villages organized six groups of hunters into co-operatives. The RIIC then provided field-level training in the processing of skins. The development trust, in co-operation with the government Rural Industrial Officer, organized the marketing.

The village carpentry unit

The second artisan training unit to be started was in carpentry. Again, the emphasis is on self-sufficiency, with minimal external input. Trainees are taught how to identify particular indigenous trees for their timber characteristics and how to manufacture work-benches, vices and other simple equipment, so that they will be able to begin production 'under the tree', with only a few purchased tools.

As with the tannery unit, some practical research was carried out, for example on how to produce round timber products without an expensive power-driven lathe. A simple horizontal foot-powered lathe was produced at minimal cost, which can be easily 'home-made' and can run at three speeds through a stepped-pulley transmission.

The village blacksmith unit

The blacksmith unit, started in 1982, perhaps has the greatest potential, although it faces a number of problems.

Training is based on the use of local scrap materials and the trainees are first taught how to produce their own bellows and forges. They then go on to make basic blacksmith's tools including tongs, punches, hammers and the like.

After doing two courses, the village blacksmith will have a wide range of skills and potential products. He will be able to make axes, knives, adzes, rakes, hoes, spades, picks, hammers, buckets, stoves and trunks, as well as being able to make parts for agricultural implements. He will also be able to produce a range of simple low-cost transport items including wheelbarrows, handcarts and donkey carts using a special 'no welds' design.

However, one of the most important functions of the barefoot blacksmith is his ability to provide back-up support in repairs and maintenance to agricultural equipment. The government's Arable Lands Development Programme (ALDEP) aims at providing a package of inputs, techniques and services to increase the productivity of those farmers who try to operate at slightly above subsistence level. As part of the package, thousands of animal-drawn ploughs, planters and harrows have been made available to farmers on a subsidized basis. It was soon realized that in remote land areas there was no back-up service available. In fact, even before the ALDEP programme started, anybody who lived in rural Botswana was familiar with the sight of a plough or other piece of agricultural equipment lying idle under a tree, only because of the lack of a few bolts or other simple spares.

The 'modern sector' distribution network for spares and repairs does not reach these areas and would be unable to do so on an economic basis. However, the barefoot blacksmith, who is often himself a farmer in years of good rains, can provide these services at low cost and manufacture many parts which are unavailable locally. A number of studies have shown that lack of either draft power or primary tillage equipment in good order during the critically short period prior to and during the rains leads to either a failure to plant on the part of many, or to untimely planting with a lower chance of success. The village blacksmith training unit is effectively addressing at least one of these problems.

Problems and constraints

Although it is six years since the RIIC started its first artisan training unit, the tannery, the organization was at that time suffering from a severe lack of human and financial resources and activities started gradually on a very small scale. As resources improved, so did both the quality of training and the number of trainees, so that by 1983-4 the Centre was training as many as 200 people each year, more or less evenly divided between the basic and upgrading courses.

There began to be increasing evidence that many of the ex-trainees were not going into production or using their skills. Apparently this was for reasons other than saturation of the market. As a result the number of trainees has now been reduced, with increased emphasis on 'follow-through'.

Botswana has a bewildering abundance of small business support services and also many sources of capital, including government grants. It was initially assumed that if the technical skills could be provided, together with some 'linking' assistance from the RIIC Extension Team, this would be sufficient for the graduates to get into business with the support from this large network of existing agencies. There has also been some tendency to duplicate services already offered, so that RIIC had been reluctant to get into business education or financial support. However, it is now clear that simply providing the technical skills and a few tools is not enough and RIIC is therefore moving towards the provision of some of these services on an experimental basis.

A modest start was made in 1985 when RIIC ran a joint course with 'Partnership for Productivity', a non-government agency that provides business advice and micro-financing, mainly for the informal sector. This was not entirely successful, as the trainees proved highly motivated in acquiring the technical skills, but not very enthusiastic about the business advice. Such advice will probably prove more effective in future if it can be provided in the field rather than at the Centre, so there are plans to equip extension staff with the necessary skills.

Although small-scale grant financing is theoretically easily available for the small rural producer through the government's 'Financial Assistance Programme' (FAP), such grants may in practice take six months or more to process and the applicant also has to provide a certain percentage from his or her own resources, which is often impossible. RIIC is therefore introducing a pilot scheme whereby those trainees who show the greatest promise are given the equivalent of about $100 in tools and materials immediately on completion of training. This could also be counted as an 'own contribution' and will enable them to get into business on a very small scale whilst awaiting further support from FAP.

Future directions

In 1987, in addition to introducing some new units such as the barefoot chemists who will be able to make candles, soap and allied products, RIIC was planning to undertake two major initiatives to address the problems faced by the present training units in getting its graduates into production.

First, there will be a detailed follow-up study of 50 ex-trainees to identify the constraints they are facing in getting into business. Through the existing follow-up work and from a seminar of ex-trainees held in 1986, there is already an indication of what some of the problems may be. For example, the blacksmith training is based on the use of scrap material, mainly from vehicles, but this is not always readily available in remote locations. It is hoped that this follow-up survey will provide a more detailed and systematic analysis.

Second, using the best of the ex-trainees from the blacksmith unit, it is planned to establish seven blacksmith 'mini-centres' around the country, with full initial support provided, including a simple workshop, tools and equipment, and working capital. By monitoring these units very closely it is expected that operational problems and requirements for extra technical, business or other assistance will be identified more quickly. The physical facilities will remain the property of RIIC until the blacksmith can prove himself, and then will be handed over to the entrepreneur in exchange for his continued support to RIIC initiatives in training and in transfer of technology. The 'mini-centres' can also be used as a testing ground for new products designed by RIIC for eventual incorporation into the training programme.

The next few years are likely to be troubled ones in Southern Africa. It is hoped that the establishment of the village artisan training approach on a firmer foundation will, in a small way, help Botswana to become more economically self-sufficient. It is also possible that some of the lessons learnt may be of benefit to the other neighbouring 'frontline states'.

MECHANICS IN INDIA — VILLAGE-LEVEL HANDPUMP MAINTENANCE IN ACTION

Sanjit Roy

The effectiveness of any idea lies in its simplicity. In situations where government involvement is marginal and the expertise of the technocrat almost non-existent, and where the technical and human resources available in the village are utilized to the full, ideas put into practice have worked. More importantly, they have continued to receive community sanction.

When high-powered engineers put their heads together over any scheme involving rural people, one does not have to look too far for failures. Engineers have not been trained to appreciate or accept the very real skills and expertise of the community. Invariably, their involvement results in simple ideas being translated into something which looks complicated, extravagantly expensive and terrifyingly technical.

This is exactly what happened when the UNICEF-designed Three-Tier System of repairing and maintaining handpumps was approved by technocrats of all the State Governments in India at the National Conference on Deep-well Handpumps held in Madurai in July 1979.

The Three-Tier System

The Three-Tier System is supposed to work as follows:

Tier 1
At village level, there is a handpump caretaker. (S)he is selected by the government, works free of charge, is trained periodically, is given spanners to keep nuts and bolts tight, and is supposed to keep the foundation clean.

Tier 2
At block-level (100 villages), there is an inspector-cum-mechanic of the Government Public Health Engineering Department who is responsible for checking 50 handpumps and carrying out minor

repairs above the ground. These workers have no transport provided, and if handpump assembly has to be taken out, the District Maintenance Unit has to be called.

Tier 3

At district level, there is a Mobile Maintenance Team (one for every 500 handpumps) consisting of five workers (driver, mechanic, mason, two helpers). This team works under the supervision of a Junior Engineer. Almost no training is given to these teams, and yet they are supposed to attend to all major and minor repairs.

It took the rural people — the barefoot mechanics of the world — to point out how absurd and flawed this Three-Tier System was. First, it presumed that rural people had no skills themselves and that urban skills had to be 'imported'. Second, it presumed that rural people had no knowledge and experience and that it required someone with paper qualifications to repair and maintain an India Mark II handpump. The designers of the system failed to notice and take account of the fact that illiterate men and women in the region were already making a living from repairing much more sophisticated equipment such as electric and diesel pumps and tractors.

The One-Tier System

The alternative idea of the One-Tier System based on a Handpump Mechanic (HPM) grew out of discussions with the users of the Three-Tier System who were tired of waiting for someone from the government to arrive to repair their pump. Simple people got together and said, 'if we can repair our electric and diesel pumps, tractors and bullock carts, what is so difficult about repairing handpumps?'

After much discussion with the communities, several practical ideas were incorporated in the One-Tier System:

○ the identification of rural youth from economically poor backgrounds with mechanical aptitudes whose skills could be upgraded through training under TRYSEM (Training of Rural Youth for Self-Employment), a Government-approved scheme operational all over India;
○ the mobilization of government resources to pay stipends to these HPMs while they are being trained for three months under TRYSEM;
○ the placement of trained HPMs in villages where they are

accountable to the community rather than to a government department;
○ the provision of credit by banks for the purchase of tools so that, in due course, the HPMs can be self-supporting;
○ the location of over 1,000 fully-trained HPMs to look after 30,000 handpumps in the State, thus reducing government expenditure, minimizing official influence and control and handing over maintenance and repair of rural water supplies to communities

The sooner engineers and policy makers (including international organizations like UNICEF) realize that handpump maintenance is no longer a technical problem but a social one, the One-Tier System can be seriously considered as one answer to many of the serious problems facing rural India. While the Government wants to decentralize and let community assets be maintained by the community, there has been no collective move by any Central or State government to convince the community that the assets belong to the community, *not* the Government.

The One-Tier System addresses the problem of unemployment among rural youth, making them feel useful and generating self-respect. It has also enabled the community to be less dependent on government, thus promoting self-reliance.

The Handpump Mechanics

When the scheme was first introduced on a small scale in Ajmer District, it was supported by UNICEF. However, when plans were made to replicate the scheme throughout the State of Rajasthan in place of the Three-Tier System, there was some opposition from UNICEF and government engineers who were uncertain that an HPM could do the job of a caretaker, a block mechanic and 90 per cent of the work of a District Maintenance Unit.

In Ajmer District, the profiles of 71 HPMs were studied in depth. Some of the characteristics of these HPMs are outlined in Table 5.

What is interesting about the HPMs is the fact that they come from very humble backgrounds. One of them, Satish Chandra Purohit, from Srinagar Village, was born in 1951 and went to school for 15 years before leaving to help his father on the farm. Later he worked as a cleaner, then as a mason, and later as a part-time motor mechanic. He now looks after 30 handpumps within a radius of five kilometres from his village.

Another HPM, Shareef Khan, studied until eighth standard and then worked as a cleaner on a truck and as a coolie in a railway station; now, he looks after 40 handpumps.

Table 5: Characteristics of handpump mechanics in Ajmer District, Rajasthan

	No
Occupational Status	
Agricultural labourers	51
Famine workers	8
Blacksmiths	2
Cycle repair shops	2
Other	8
Land Holdings	
Landless	19
Up to 2.5 acres	34
3 to 6 acres	16
Over 6 acres	2
Income other than from HPM work (Rs/month)	
Rs50 — Rs100	30
Rs101 — Rs150	31
Rs151 — Rs200	10
Educational qualifications	
Up to 5th standard	29
6th to 7th standard	35
8th to 10th standard	6
Over 10th standard	1

Ayadan Kumar from Jethana village studied until tenth standard and owns three acres of land. His father is a village potter. When he is not repairing handpumps, he helps his father.

Kailash Chandra from Kharwa Village studied until eighth standard. He belongs to a scheduled caste, owns 0.5 acres of land and looks after 30 handpumps. Amar Bal Bhambhi from Loharwada village is also from a scheduled caste. He was too poor to carry on his studies after eighth standard and worked in a lime kiln and as an agricultural labourer. He now looks after 48 handpumps.

Satyanarain dropped out from school because he had to help his father who is a dyer by profession. He worked for three years in a cotton mill in Ahmedabad, which is 300 miles from his village. He returned to his village when he lost his job because of illness. He now looks after 36 handpumps.

Shankar Lal from Sursura village has no land. He has four brothers and two sisters and his family's monthly income is only Rs200 per month. He works as a barber, but the money he earns from looking after 40 handpumps provides additional income which is badly needed in the family.

These are ordinary profiles of extraordinary people who have contributed a great deal to their country but who would have been rejected by conventional western norms.

Secrets of success

A major factor in the success of the One-Tier System is that the HPMs have a stake in making it work since they are answerable to their communities and are concerned about earning self-respect in their villages.

As opposed to the Three-Tier System, where the caretaker is totally dependent on the block mechanic and the District Mobile Maintenance Unit, the One-Tier System enables the HPM to be almost totally self-reliant. Properly trained, the HPMs can carry out all minor and most major repairs on their own.

While the Three-Tier System fails to take the community into confidence, the One-Tier System cannot work without community support. In the Three-Tier System, if no-one wants to work, there is nothing the community can do about it. In the One-Tier System, the HPMs have to get a certificate from the Village Headman that the pumps are functioning properly before they are paid by the government. If the HPM does not work efficiently, the community can select someone else and send them for training. This fear alone makes most HPMs work hard.

Comparative analysis

A comparison between the Three-Tier and One-Tier Systems is outlined in the following Tables. Table 6 looks at the socio-economic characteristics of the two systems; Table 7 gives a technical comparison.

Constraints

Probably the greatest threat to the scheme's continued success is the bias of the engineers and other professionals who are convinced that the rural poor are illiterate, primitive and socially inferior and cannot handle handpump maintenance themselves.

Many of the problems experienced in the One-Tier System can be traced to this lack of confidence in rural people. For example, in many places the bank manager will not sanction loans to the HPMs because he feels they will run off with the cash. In any case, his sympathy is with the engineers.

Hope for the future

In Amjer District the mechanics have now grouped together and registered the first co-operative of its kind in India. They are

Table 6: Three-Tier and One-Tier Systems: A Socio-economic comparison

Socio-economic Indicators	Three-Tier system	One-Tier system
Cost/handpump/year to maintain	Rs1,000/handpump/year	Rs250/handpump/year, with Rs50 included for spare parts per handpump per year
Tools and equipment	Trucks, jeeps, trailers, heavy repair equipment, special tools etc	Cycle, special tools
Educational qualifications	Mechanical Degree Holder ITI Diploma	4th-10th standard pass; primary school leaver adequate
Personnel	Additional Chief Engineer, Superintendent Engineer, Executive Engineer, Assistant Engineer, Junior Engineer, Block Mechanics, Caretakers, other lower staff eg masons, drivers etc	Handpump mechanic at village level
Training	No long-term systematic programme at any level. Only short-term orientation course periodically	3 months' training under TRYSEM 2 months' field training and 1 month theory. Identification of handpumps they will repair is part of training
Community participation	Marginal at the caretaker level only	HPM identified and selected by the community: priority given to lower castes and person living below the poverty line
Community accountability	None. Answerable only to government	The users have the right to recall the HPM and send someone else for training if his work is poor
Community resources	No use of village resources	The use of village knowledge, experience and skills are total
Institutional finance	No provision. Tools are given free to caretakers	HPMs take a loan from the nearest bank of Rs2,500 for special tools. Subsidy of 50% if the HPM is from a scheduled caste

Table 7: Three-Tier and One-Tier Systems: A technical comparison

Description of Fault	Three-Tier system			One-Tier system	
	Category Major/Minor	Responsibility		Category	Responsibility
1. Above Ground (Mechanical)					
Tightening of nuts and bolts (flange nuts and others)	Minor	Caretaker		Minor	HPM
Replacement of nuts and bolts	Minor	Block fitter		Minor	HPM
Service of bearing or replacement	Minor	District Maintenance Unit (DMU)		Minor	HPM
Repairing of chain or replacement	Minor	DMU		Minor	HPM
Rethreading connecting rod (above ground)	Minor	DMU		Minor	HPM
Replacement of any other part above ground	Minor	DMU		Minor	HPM
2. Foundation Work					
Repairing of platform	Major	DMU		Minor	HPM with help of community
Construction of new platform	Major	DMU		Minor	HPM
3. Below Ground					
Disconnecting of delivery pipes	Major	DMU		Minor	HPM
Rethreading of pipe	Major	DMU		Minor	HPM
Disconnection of connecting rod (CR)	Major	DMU		Minor	HPM
Rethreading of CR below ground	Major	DMU		Minor	HPM
Any other repair in pipe/CR	Major	DMU		Minor	HPM
Cylinder repair	Major	DMU		Minor	HPM
Fishing of whole assembly	Major	DMU		Minor	HPM has taken it out himself many times
Taking out whole assembly (stuck in roots/wrong)	Major	DMU		Minor	HPM taken out whole assembly with locally available materials
Bore hole development	Major	DMU		Major	HPM with government drilling team

prepared to take the responsibility for identifying handpump mechanics, giving them training, monitoring their performance and disbursing funds according to the number of operational handpumps. The engineers are obviously opposed to this proposal and it is still under debate.

Hopefully, it is only a question of time before the idea of the HPM becomes respectable in the eyes of the bureaucracy: the community accepted it years ago.

BUILDERS IN IRAN, GUINEA AND THE SUDAN — THE BAREFOOT APPROACH TO SHELTER

John Norton

In 1977 fourteen builders from Selseleh took part in a training programme in Yazd, Iran, organized and run by the Development Workshop[1] as part of its three-year involvement with the Selseleh Integrated Development Project (SIDP).

The people in the Selseleh area in Luristan, Western Iran, by tradition predominantly nomads living in tents, had in recent years been increasingly obliged to turn to a more settled way of living for which they lacked experience and for which the area was ill-equipped. The aim of the project was to help these inhabitants achieve better living conditions and it operated in two ways. One involved training young men and women from the villages so that they could undertake basic health education and care for the villagers, teach both the adults and the children to read and write and provide assistance for agriculture and animal husbandry. The other involved the provision of basic services and infrastructure, such as roads, water supply, public baths, clinics, schools and the development of activities which could provide both building materials for the area and opportunities for employment.

The training of a team of builders similar to the village trainees responsible for health, education or agriculture, was seen by Development Workshop as an essential part of the overall development of the region and therefore an addition that would enhance the project. The builders' role included building and maintaining the public facilities in the community, and providing assistance to individual householders; members of the family provided the semi-skilled labour, with the paid assistance of the village builder, who provided specialist skills. These builders were ideally placed to contribute to an improvement in the quality of shelter in the area and the way in which families built and maintained their homes. They were the people who both understood the local conditions and were able at the same time to benefit from a training programme and to pass on any innovation and improvement in their skill to the individual households. The builders' training programme was therefore designed both to increase their awareness of local building needs and of the materials and techniques which could be used to solve them and to equip them with the organizational and practical skills that would enable them to meet these needs.

Although some of the participants in the training programme had only a limited experience of building, all of them had varying but invaluable knowledge of their own region, of the basic resources and how they had been used in the past, and of the social and economic circumstances of the inhabitants. Recognizing that successful and acceptable solutions to building problems can only be developed in the context of this local knowledge, each aspect of the training programme was developed on the basis of sharing and evaluating the experience of *all* the participants including both the trainees and the

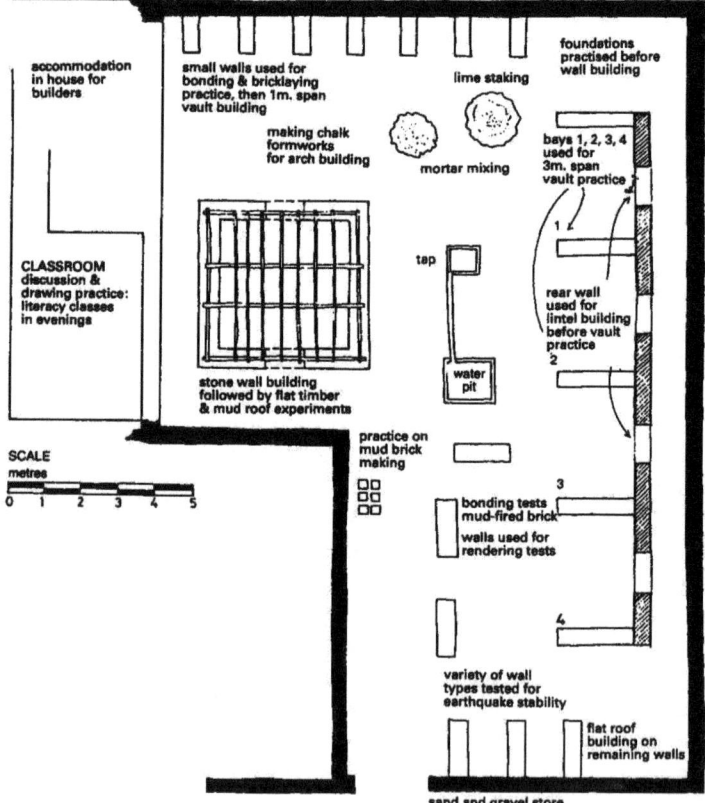

Fig. 1 Plan of the Yazd training site, with the location of different activities

members of Development Workshop running the programme. Problems and ideas were discussed and the possible ways of meeting the building needs and exploiting the potentials of the Selseleh area were agreed collectively. Each technique was then tested and developed through practical work and experimentation in the building yard of the training site (Fig. 1).

As the basis for the whole programme, the trainee builders were asked to identify the resources and potentials and the shortages and problems in the Selseleh area. Through the discussion of how the resources could be used to deal with the problems, the participants were able to outline a strategy for the development of the region. This strategy included ideas about how the local resources could be developed to provide the necessary building materials for the area, to what extent people in the area would be able to meet their own building needs and in what ways external help was required. The builders were able to see that where people in the region encountered problems related to building and shelter, it was they themselves who were best placed to provide assistance. Therefore they needed to operate not only as local builders but also as community or 'barefoot architects', capable of providing advice on how to lay out a building, what sort of foundations, walls or roof would be needed and how this could be achieved safely and economically. At the same time, if they were to take on the public building requirements of the community, they also needed to develop skills in organizing labour, ordering materials and understanding the plans and sections of small public-facility buildings which might be provided by the local authorities.

To prepare the builders for this role, the training programme introduced the basic concepts of plans and sections, firstly with the help of large models and then by practising drawing their own homes. This led to teaching methods for dimensioning their drawings and using a scale. To complement the drawing exercises, literacy classes were held in the evenings for those builders who could not read. The classes were related directly to building, such as reading notes on drawings, and this provided the builders with a professional incentive to learn. The various elements of a building were then dealt with and in each case the basic requirement or function was discussed, as well as the principles involved, and then, from this analysis, a variety of solutions were investigated. This was followed by physical demonstration and opportunities for everyone to practise the selected techniques. In some cases this meant building up and knocking down the same structure until an acceptable standard was achieved, whilst in others a single demonstration was sufficient to provide a good example. As well as dealing with building techniques, the programme also developed skills in evaluating the suitability of a building site and simple analysis of soils.

After three months' training the builders returned to the Selseleh area, where winter was over and a new building season was starting. The training programme was not, however, envisaged as a finite event, but as the beginning of a process where they could go on developing their own skills and the skills of other people in the area. Sharing knowledge amongst themselves had formed one important aspect of the training programme and the builders had been encouraged to continue this practice. An immediate effect of the training programme was seen in the improved quality of work being done by these builders, on public buildings which formed part of the SIDP activities, and on private domestic work which they took on as well. Techniques such as the use of low arches over window openings which had been tried out and accepted in the training programme began to appear in homes in the area. With their increased skill, the builders were working faster, but they were also taking on an increasing amount of the building work in the Selseleh area. With this responsibility came the need to find more people to assist them in meeting the local building needs. Just over a year after the first builders' training programme run by Development Workshop, the original trainee builders themselves organized a second training session, sponsored by the SIDP, to go over the ground they had covered and to pass on knowledge to a new group of trainees.

The builder as an agent of development

If some of the circumstances in which the programme described above took place appear exceptional, it is worth considering how common the situation actually is in most of the less developed world. Individual families are the people most directly involved in and responsible for the process of acquiring their own shelter. In the past, most of the domestic and communal building needs made use of local resources and drew from the store of local knowledge of building techniques. These techniques have typically been built up through centuries of experience and the results have in many cases been extremely successful, capable of producing a comfortable environment within the limits of the materials and money available, with little need of help from people outside the community. Although most families had some knowledge of building, enough perhaps to produce a basic shelter, they often relied upon the local professional builders in the community for expert guidance and it is these builders who held and passed on the accumulated experience of local building methods. The common relationship on the domestic building site in many developing countries remains that of the hired builder working with one or two apprentices and the support of the family for whom the house is being built, who provide the unskilled labour.

In recent decades the demand for the various types of shelter needed by a community, including both houses and public buildings such as schools, clinics and workshops, has progressively increased as populations and aspirations grow. Local ability to meet this demand, using the traditional methods and skills which served in the past, has frequently decreased as a result of the changing circumstances in which people find themselves living. Some of the clearest examples of these changing circumstances are found in the urban areas, where increasingly high population densities and the subsequent concentrated demand for materials, land and services make the process of achieving shelter more difficult. Similarly in the rural areas there are examples of change in life style, a change from a nomadic to a sedentary life, desertification or new land uses, all of which can alter the suitability and availability of techniques and materials which have been used in the past to meet shelter needs. At the same time as such circumstances may be changing, people are also in many cases hoping for a higher standard of living, better status and, in more specific terms, looking to use more durable materials and have better services.

Faced with this growing demand, and in some instances a need for innovation to cope with new circumstances, the ability and capacity of governments and qualified organizations and individuals to provide people with a better built environment, or to help them directly in achieving it themselves, is frequently limited. This is firstly because the amount of assistance which is needed is enormous and, by comparison, there are only a small number of qualified people — architects, engineers, planners, technicians and similar — who are available to help and secondly because the priorities, needs, aspirations and means of each individual family or community are extremely variable and often only well understood by people working closely within the community.

In this situation the local builder is placed in a potentially special position. He knows the people and conditions of his own community and he knows the materials and techniques which have been used traditionally for the different types of local building. He is accepted by the families in his community as the person who can give advice and provide those skills which a family building their own house might not possess and through this experience he usually knows what may be both acceptable and affordable in the community.

Thus changes to existing building practices are needed, the local builder is the one person who is well placed both to be trained in any new technique and to help to diffuse it through the community. He can become the local 'agent' for building development, providing a service to the people in the community and paid for by each individual family building their house and employing his assistance. But, respecting his knowledge of the local conditions, the local builder should also have a role in identifying the need for any innovation and in ensuring that any new ideas and techniques do actually correspond to a local potential to make use of them. A training programme to improve quality or to introduce a new skill or material in order to overcome a building problem needs therefore to be organized to encourage a two-way exchange of ideas between the trainers and the trainees, similar to that which took place with the Selseleh builders, where everyone had something to contribute.

Earthquake assistance through builders' training

This approach of using the local builders as the diffusers of improvement or innovation can be applied to specific problems as well as to a general improvement in the quality of the built environment. An example of this occurred in Guinea, West Africa. In 1983 an earthquake destroyed or damaged most of the houses in the area around Koumbia, in the remote north-west corner of the country. Over 5,000 houses needed to be replaced. The government did not have the resources necessary to rebuild the damaged houses, and in any case the local people would in the long run need to go on building their own homes with the materials available in the area and without external assistance. The problem was to ensure that the inhabitants would be able to build both then and in the future with techniques which would make their buildings more earthquake resistant and which at the same time they could afford. Development Workshop were invited to assess the earthquake damage and to organize a programme of assistance for the rebuilding of the area. There were too many villages for it to have been practical to provide direct assistance to each affected family and therefore a builders' training programme was organized, culminating in the construction of several houses to demonstrate suitable earthquake-resistant building techniques.

The participants were all builders or carpenters who volunteered to take part in the programme and who were paid at the normal rate for building work. Usually they earned their living either by taking on a contract to build a house for someone or, when the client was poor, by working with members of the family. They would thus be able to pass on to others any new techniques.

The traditional buildings in the area were for the most part round houses, with thatched roofs. The walls were thin, and built up either with mud-blocks or with a wood and bamboo lattice over which mud was plastered. In the earthquake, the mud-block walls had proved very unstable and many had collapsed, causing damage and injury. On the other hand, the lattice and mud walls, which were potentially stable, had frequently been badly weakened before the earthquake by termites, and therefore suffered damage as well. In the training programme, Development Workshop suggested that the earthquake resistance of the walls could be improved by combining the load-bearing strength of mud-blocks with a bamboo lattice to provide stability when shaken by a tremor. In order, however, to overcome the termite problem, the bamboo should be placed on both the inside and outside surfaces of the mud-block wall (Fig. 2) where they could be checked and replaced when they had been damaged by termites. During the programme, this idea was then evolved with the builders into a system which they found workable and attractive. Their contribution meant that in some cases materials were changed, because the builders felt that they would be difficult for the average family to obtain and in others there were alterations and elaborations to the technique to suit local habits. The result was a building method which increased earthquake ⁓resistance but which scarcely altered either the basic form of the houses in the area or their cost. After six weeks of supervised work four demonstration houses using local materials were structurally complete and the builders were ready to complete four more houses in other villages and begin their task of disseminating the technique through working with individual families.

Turning development workers into builders

In both the examples described so far, there has been a tradition of local builders working with and for the individual families in the community and providing specialist skills. There are, however, many situations where the clear role of a local builder does not exist and where building is a part-time activity of people engaged in other activities as well. Help in house building is often provided at best by neighbours and friends in exchange for a meal. The poorer the community, the more likely this is to be the situation. To develop the skills of these part-time builders may be valuable but it does not necessarily lead to the development of people who can provide a service of improved building expertise to the community. One aspect of a training programme run by Development Workshop[2] in Southern Sudan in 1984 took an alternative approach. Community development workers with a background of working closely with people in a community, but paid by the government, took part in the six-week training programme. They already had experience of finding out what the problems were in a community, of helping the people to find solutions to them and of mobilizing the community to undertake

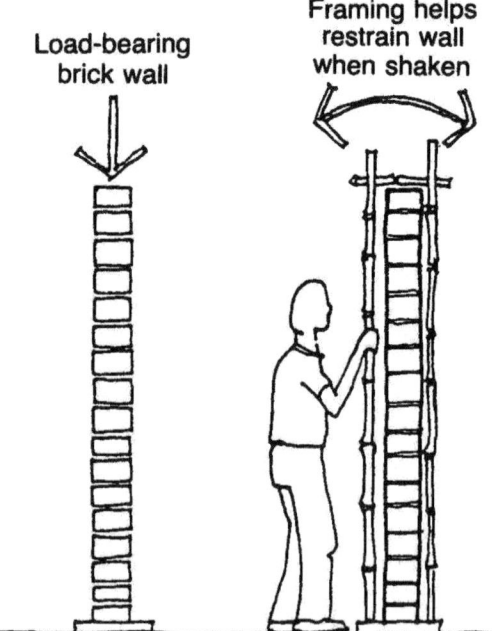

Fig. 2 Illustration from the training manual showing the arrangement of the bamboo framework and the mud-block wall

larger projects but, lacking knowledge of building, they were handicapped in assisting people to improve their own homes or in ensuring that the public building provided examples of how such improvement could be achieved. In the training programme, these community development workers learned about the functions of the different elements of a building, how the various locally available materials could be used to achieve these functions and which ones to use in various circumstances. Discussion included how to select a site, draw plans and lay out the building. Theoretical knowledge was then supported by practical work on a building site and the programme ended with the construction of a primary school with community assistance. The actual involvement in producing the materials and building with them, as well as in organizing the building process, helped to bring the trainees closer to the realities and difficulties of construction. This process in turn improved their ability to explain and demonstrate a variety of techniques in response to the needs of members of the community with whom they would be working.

Building on local knowledge

Underlying the examples given here is a recognition that the majority of shelter in poorer communities will continue to be built by individual families making use of their own resources and with little help from outside the community. This process is often informal and makes use of techniques and materials which may have little in common with the norms of more formal building activity. The need for assistance to bring improvements to the quality of shelter in these communities is rarely in question, but the way in which this assistance can usefully be provided needs to take into account that the options available to those most in need are frequently very limited, and are as often controlled by factors such as poverty or insecurity as by lack of technical know-how. The need for an understanding of these limitations is one of the considerations that favour the development of building skills from within the community and, where this is not directly possible, at least with people working on a long-term basis with the community. At the same time, this approach is an efficient and cheap way of extending useful assistance to a large number of people.

In organizing the training of local builders to assume a broader role in the acquisition of good shelter and services within the community, the aim should be to exploit and add to their existing knowledge so that they can both provide better quality and bring to each problem a wider range of possible solutions. The training should encourage them to develop their own conclusions about which techniques and materials will best meet the local building needs and, to complement this, it should develop their organizational skills to enable them to take on more substantial projects in their community.

Training community development workers to have a better understanding of building problems and solutions carries with it the risk of imposing values or techniques which are not then readily adopted by the community. Their training therefore calls for the development of a good sensitivity to the indigenous built environment. It should promote an aptitude for practical work and, most of all, the habit of working alongside the part-time builders in the community so that both can learn from each other.

In either case it is frequently extremely helpful to support the efforts of these trained builders and community development workers by the production of manuals and documentation relevant to the techniques they are using and developed to suit their levels of literacy and familiarity with drawn images.[3] Further support to the development of the role of the community builders can be provided through periodic programmes of review and revision, to bring them up to date with any new techniques relevant to their local context and to provide an opportunity to discuss any difficulties that they may be facing. This in turn begins to define a role for the architects, engineers and planners, not so much to provide instructions but to support the activities of the community builder with assistance and advice.

In poorer communities, the builders and part-time builders will remain the people most involved in solving the problems of shelter. It makes sense to help them improve their work and to place them in a position to draw upon new ideas and innovate within the context of their building tradition to meet the rapidly changing needs of their community.

GEOLOGISTS IN SRI LANKA — THE BAREFOOT APPROACH TO NATURAL RESOURCE DEVELOPMENT

Michael Katz

Deliberations on geoscience education in developing countries have stressed the importance of strengthening universities and other specialist-level training centres to produce more professional geologists. There is a tendency to strive for and support geoscience education to the highest, élitest levels, but little data is available to suggest that this direction is the right, or most useful and relevant path.

This approach has produced many capable scientists in developing countries and many national and international organizations have fostered this group by encouraging and supporting further élitist-type ventures, meetings and training courses. There is no doubt as to the value of these projects in terms of satisfying the needs of this small community, but does the impact of these projects trickle down to the fundamental development problems of resource assessment and environmental impact or to areas where geology can contribute to the provision of basic human needs?

The costs involved in training and sustaining these geoscientific élitist groups are very high and the benefits are not necessarily commensurate with the costs. International organizations must continue their support of the professional geoscientific communities in developing countries. However, they must also take the initiative and spread their support to lower technical and sub-technical levels of activity, especially to the uneducated, rural villager.

For example, villagers could play a very important role as 'barefoot' geologists or prospectors/artisanal miners in locating a wide range of potential resources. Individual prospectors/miners have located many metallic mineral resources in Canada, the USA, Australia, Finland and elsewhere and in Japan there is a long history of non-metallic prospecting/mining. Individual prospectors discovered the copper deposits of southern Peru, iron ore in the Nimba mountains of West Africa and diamonds in Tanzania. These groups of prospectors can be encouraged, supported, and trained at a very low cost and with potentially very high returns. Training courses could run at a fraction of the costs of training professionals.

Villager herdsmen have an intimate, instinctive knowledge of their environment and they are aware of the topography, water holes, rock types and, consciously or otherwise, monitor for volcanic activity, landslides, earthquakes, floods and other natural hazards. These rural people often set up cottage industries in quarrying, ornamental and gem stones, rock crafts and building stones and they are keenly aware of rocks of unusual colour, lustre, density, breakage and shaping properties. Thus they can, with little training, be converted into village geologists trained in prospecting for economic, industrial and fertilizer minerals, energy and water resources.

The village prospector

Meetings and papers on resource exploration and small-scale mining in developing countries increasingly refer to the potential role that villagers can play as prospectors and a strong case can be made for making prospector education an important and critical responsibility of a geological survey. During surveys in various parts of the country the local villagers, herdsmen and even tribesmen could be encouraged to participate in survey activities and at the same time be trained in elementary prospecting/mining techniques. Ideally, when the survey completes its work it should leave behind trained cadres of prospectors that could continue their prospecting with promises of substantial rewards if they find anything. Tamale-Ssali, a pioneer Ugandan geologist on exploration strategy, proposed that the general public be involved in a mineral exploration militia. The geological survey could accommodate this programme without any particular increase in general cost or time and although the programme would be scattered and sporadic, it would be concentrated in mineral-potential areas. Gaps in this programme could be filled by university field research groups where staff and students' investigations in remote areas would also have a compulsory element of training local prospectors. An example of this type of co-operation comes from a small-scale mining project in the Mkomazi village, Tanzania.

However, geological surveys in developing countries, with few exceptions, do not have prospector education programmes. In

India, neither the Geological Survey of India nor other government agencies offer any incentives to prospectors, although the Survey has launched programmes for making laymen mineral-conscious by a series of demonstrations and lectures in remote parts of the country. Proposed courses for prospectors in Kenya are being developed by the Earth Science Technical Education Project of the Kenya Polytechnic.

The geological societies could also play an important role here by publicizing these programmes of training and educating the rural populations to be aware of the mineral, water and energy resource potential of their areas, as well as the problems related to the environment and local natural hazards. Obviously, state mining corporations and even the multinational companies should be encouraged to support these training programmes. These prospector training schemes can be an important and vital complementary activity to the more sophisticated and modern techniques of resource exploration carried out by these companies. In some countries, regional centres of prospecting training or local schools of mines, possibly modelled on the Haileybury School of Mines, Canada could be established to formalize the training on a more technical level and these schools could be located in well-known mineral centres (eg, Recuay Mining School in Peru).

A Mineral Prospectors' Training Programme has been undertaken in Uganda with the co-operation of the Uganda Geological Survey, and low-cost, practical, non-prestigious projects such as this are the kind of thing that should be supported. The Finnish experience of using amateur prospectors could be very useful in developing countries. Similarly, a lead could be taken from the self-reliant approach of the Chinese in their science and technology, which has developed the well-known 'barefoot seismologist', trained in monitoring and predicting earthquakes. This could be furthered in the search for mineral, energy and water resources.

The village geoscientist

Although there is still a need for prospecting for valuable commodities in developing countries, the present-day metal glut and low prices place commodity-dependent developing countries in an economic crisis. The developing countries' resource needs have changed in the last few years and a more broad resource-based background is required on all levels of national development and conservation. This changing role of geosciences in development must be taken into account in the training of the village geoscientist. This includes the search for industrial and fertilizer minerals, salts, building and ceramic materials, alternative energy sources, clean and reliable water resources, as well as training in the mitigation of geological and environmental hazards, the 'ten geological plagues':

- Drought
- Flood
- Land erosion
- Coastal erosion
- Silting
- Subsidence
- Landslide
- Soil instability
- Volcanism
- Earthquake

In arid lands there is the major problem of desertification that also requires urgent geoscientific input to educate the masses on allaying erosion and land-use mismanagement. One such changing role of geosciences in development is the important and relevant application of geology to soil improvement using locally available rock material (agrogeology). The highly leached soils of the tropics are often deficient in minor nutrients and trace elements and have not been naturally rejuvenated by volcanism, sedimentation or other geological processes that add fresh rock to these highly weathered soils and increase the fertility of the land. In much of Africa, South America and parts of Asia where these natural processes have not been active on a large scale, a possible strategy for maintaining the fertility of the land would be to use common and readily available rocks as fertilizers.

The trends in developing countries for urbanization and the inherent problems that eventuate may now require geoscientific education among the poor masses so that they will be able to understand the urban geological environment, especially in regard to water management and pollution. All these factors are raised to make the geoscientific educational programme as complete, relevant and up to date as possible. The tasks are enormous, but a start in this direction, which could have some immediate and tangible results, would be a village geologist training programme for an appropriate, small-scale, community-based cottage industry level of involvement, that could, in the first instance, concentrate on local industrial minerals and rocks (eg, phosphate for fertilizer), building materials (eg, sand, gravel and adobe or mud brick) and energy resources (eg, peat and low-grade coal deposits).

Sri Lanka: an example

Geology and geological processes influence the lives of all rural and urban communities in Sri Lanka in such important constructive areas as agriculture, water supply and industrial material and in potentially destructive areas such as erosion, pollution and land slips. Villagers utilizing local mineral, energy and water resources are a common sight, even to the casual visitor. Quarries are labour intensive and stones are sized for building, facing and paving stones, down to road metal and aggregate. Lime kilns are common in the central areas where persistent formations of marble are located. Processes such as erosion, slope instability and land slips are often observed while travelling along the roads in the Sri Lankan highlands or when visiting tea plantations and hill stations. Sojourns to the beaches highlight problems related to coastal erosion and stagnant, silted and polluted waters can be found both in the rural and urban areas.

The western half of Sri Lanka is located in a dry zone, an area of low rainfall and long periods of drought where problems of water supply are of major importance. The use of geology in siting good wells is vital for the communities in these dry areas. Unstable slopes in many areas of Sri Lanka lead to destructive and costly landslides and earth slips. Deforestation, inadequate drainage systems and the cultivation of unstable slopes by locals contribute to these disasters. Sri Lanka is largely an agricultural economy dependent on its soils. Geology controls the development and rejuvenation of soils and minerals and rock material may be used for fertilizer and soil improvement. Cottage industries in the use of clay for ceramics, stone quarrying and lime kilns are widespread and there are many local small-scale gem, graphite and mica mines. The obvious mineral, energy and water resources are usually put into traditional use, often with indigenous technology. As such the geological environment is not a complete unknown, but in most cases the use of geology for community and rural development in Sri Lanka is not maximized, many readily available resources are not utilized, and potential environmental hazards are often ignored.

Training

Large numbers of village geologists could be trained at little expense if an overall plan was developed by the educational/ geoscientific/mining organizations of the developing countries. The role of these organizations would be to set up training courses in villages and to plan and co-ordinate all field training activities. The syllabus and detailed curriculum would be formulated with the aid of the educational planning authorities with special educational aids designed for the speedy training of semi-literate/illiterate rural people. Audio-visual methods would be important, and special sets of minerals, rocks, charts, maps and other geoscientific educational tools and materials could be collected and assembled into portable kits. Recipe-type manuals and posters using material, language and drawings which are clear to the public are being developed by the Global Learning Division of UNU/ICSU (United Nations University/International Council of Scientific Unions). These kits and manuals would be distributed to the geological surveys, university field research teams, state and multinational corporations and educational institutes in rural towns and villages. The new AGID (Association of Geoscientists for International Development) Geoscience Video Education Program (GVEP) may be an important step in this direction.

In developing countries the most important resources are human resources. The rural, village populations should be encouraged and trained to monitor their own environment for potential resources, as well as other important environmental matters, such as earthquakes, floods and landslides. Some examples of useful resources are given in Table 8. If this village movement becomes operative, it would contribute to decentralization and development on a human scale and, ideally, further the ecological balance, decision-making and self-reliance on the small-scale, local level. Instead of the 'trickle down' process of development it would further the aims of those few educational pathfinders that advocate new systems and counter movements that are community based.

Conclusions

These cadres, with limited geological training to supplement their inherent awareness of the land they inhabit would be a great and important source of general geological information. Remote and unknown outcrops would be identified and access routes established, and this would assist regional mapping and inventory surveys. Sites of instability, unusual phenomena, anomalous water levels and other harbingers of possible natural and environmental disasters could be identified by these cadres and brought to the attention of the authorities. The geoscientific education of the rural people would not only be a great contribution to locating mineral, water and energy resources in order to assess their own resources potential, but would also contribute to the mitigation of natural geological hazards, increase of soil fertility and improvement of the environment.

Table 8: Some examples of useful village mineral and energy resources

Terrain	Resources	Uses
Volcanic	Pumice	Building stone
	Zeolites	Soil improver
	Hot water	Heating
Igneous/metamorphic	Cystalline rock	Building stone
	Marble	Ornamental/lime
	Dark mafic rocks	Soil improver
Sedimentary	Limestone	Lime — cement
	Coal	Energy — fuel
Weathered	Clay	Ceramics
	Laterite	Building stone
	Mud/clay	Adobe bricks
Aluvial	Gravel/sand	Construction material
Wet	Peat	Energy — fuel
Dry/coastal	Salt	Food — health

With the assistance of UN agencies, non-government organizations such as ICSU and AGID and other interested groups like the Intermediate Technology Development Group, this programme would further self-reliance and the social and economic development of these countries. The current agricultural resource development problems of raising cash crops versus food crops can also be illustrated here in terms of analogous geological resource development. Geological 'food' crops fulfil the basic needs of the community, while geological 'cash' crops can be used by the community to augment their income. 'Food' crops consist of essential fertilizer minerals and rocks, building material and potable water. 'Cash' crops can be harvested in quarries and small-scale mines and could consist of economic and precious minerals and building stone.

This alternative development direction should not be at the expense of appropriate advanced technological progress involving more sophisticated mineral exploration and other geological-based projects. It should be considered as a practical, fundamental, complementary activity.

LESSONS LEARNED
Marilyn Carr

The programmes and projects on which the case studies in this book are based have had a significant impact in one way or another at the district or national level and each in its way indicates the scope for reaching large numbers of people through the effective provision of low-cost, community-based services.

This conclusion draws on the experiences described to highlight points of general interest. First, it looks at the nature of the services themselves. Second, it examines their impact on rural poor communities. Third, it analyses the factors which contribute to the success and failure of such programmes and examines the probability of widespread replication.

Implementation of projects

The major points of interest involved in the implementation of the 'intermediate services' programmes fall into four categories. These relate to:
O the characteristics of the barefoot workers;
O the nature of the training they undergo and the back-up service they receive;
O the nature of the services they deliver;
O the way in which their services are paid for.

The barefoot worker

As can be seen from the preceeding chapters, workers who fall into the 'barefoot' category are a very diversified set of people. They range from illiterate livestock owners in India to unemployed school leavers in Kenya and university graduates in Bangladesh. Some, such as the health workers in China and the paralegals in Bangladesh, are people from and selected by the community. They serve and tend to perform services on a part-time basis. Others, such as the economists in Nepal and the bankers in Bangladesh, are full-time extension workers sent to communities by their employers. The 'vets' of Gujarat and the 'blacksmiths' of Botswana are people who were already practising their craft and have simply had their skills upgraded.

In most other cases, new skills have been introduced to generalists.

Management consultants in Kenya, bankers in Bangladesh and handpump mechanics in India are all young men and women who have dropped out of school or recently graduated. In many other cases, care has been taken to encourage the recruitment of more mature people who have less incentive to drift away from rural areas after training. In three cases — bankers in Bangladesh, lawyers in Bangladesh, and economists in Nepal — a special attempt was made to recruit female workers in recognition of the importance of rural women gaining access to these services and the difficulties faced by male workers in reaching women.

Nature of training
The ways in which 'barefoot workers' are trained also vary quite considerably. The length of training ranges from three days for vets in Gujarat to three months for economists in Nepal, builders in Iran and handpump mechanics in India and six months for bankers in Bangladesh. In some cases, training is continuous, in others it is split into separate parts with gaps in between to fit in with the other commitments of the trainees.

Some schemes, such as doctors in China and vets in Gujarat, emphasize totally decentralized training as close as possible to where trainees live. Most others have centralized training in residential courses. Even these, however, have a strong practical element, with the trainees spending much of their time outside the classroom. For example, lawyers visit registrars' offices, bankers spend much of their training period attached to a branch office and management consultants are attached to local businesses.

A common theme in all cases is the participative nature of the training. Courses in Gujarat were designed in consultation with *deshi* doctors. The syllabus for lawyers in Bangladesh has been modified according to the comments of the first batch of trainees and changes were made to the training of builders based on the trainees' own knowledge. In most cases, training has incorporated local knowledge and has taken account of local culture and circumstances.

Another common theme is the care taken in following up trainees' performance. In general, this has been of a low-key nature so that trainees are given encouragement and are not left to struggle in isolation with problems beyond their competence. This is aimed at boosting self-confidence rather than weakening it by criticizing and publicly correcting trainees. In some cases, such as lawyers in Bangladesh and management consultants in Kenya, a concerted effort has been made to gauge the reaction of communities to the work of the trainees as a basis for improvement.

Nature of services

The nature of the services offered by barefoot workers also varies considerably, with some being doers, some advisers and others catalysts.

For example, doctors and vets practise preventive and curative medicine. However, the ability of paralegals to effect a legal cure is limited and so they act mainly as advisers and arbiters.

Bankers provide credit to the rural poor, and blacksmiths and handpump mechanics provide farmers and rural communities with technical assistance. By contrast, economists and management consultants do not actually 'do' anything. Rather they assist people to gain access to the services available from others.

Financing

Most of the case studies talk at some length about the way in which 'barefoot workers' are paid for their services and most dwell on the need for self-financing systems.

In the case of doctors and vets, difficulties have been encountered in persuading workers to charge fees and communities to pay for them. Subsidies are available in the short term, but this is not seen as the long-term answer.

Fees which management consultants could charge are thought to be too low to finance their services and it is suggested that the only way to achieve a self-financing situation would be to combine such services with provision of loans. Certainly the case study on bankers in Bangladesh shows that a well-run rural credit programme can pay its own way in a relatively short period of time.

Impact of projects

The case studies talk in general terms about the impact of the 'barefoot' schemes on beneficiary communities, but the overall impression is one of an increase in understanding and greater control over living and working conditions.

Some of the studies do mention specific benefits. For example, the chapter on vets mentions the increased status realized by

Animal Health Workers and that on lawyers mentions the benefits to poor communities as a result of the 'demystification of the law'.

In the case of banking services in Bangladesh, borrowers have achieved significant gains in income of, typically, 30 per cent over a two-year period (as opposed to stationary income for non-borrowers). There has also been a reduced dependence on moneylenders and traders, increased participation of the landless in village politics and a general raising of self-confidence.

Local businesses found improvements after the provision of the services of management consultants, to the extent that they were willing to pay for the previously free service.

The handpump mechanic scheme in India has resulted in increased employment and self-respect for the village youths. It has also led to increased control by the community and a reduced dependence of the community on government.

Factors in success . . . and failure

Several factors can be identified as assisting in or impeding the successful implementation of the projects.

The first relates to the support that government and local authorities give to the barefoot approach and to the attitudes of local leaders and the educated élite. For example, barefoot doctors succeeded in China because of the official support the scheme received at all levels, but the barefoot economist scheme in Ecuador failed because of government opposition to people planning their own development through community committees.

The barefoot vet scheme owed much of its success to its acceptance by the authorities and to the lack of resistance from government vets. By contrast, the handpump mechanics' scheme in India is being jeopardized by the professional bias of government engineers and bank managers.

A second factor relates to the extent to which a barefoot scheme responds to a real need identified by the community itself. For example, the barefoot vets' schemes were popular with communities which were anxious to spare themselves a journey of several days to the nearest veterinary facility. The barefoot blacksmiths' scheme responded to the need for an immediate repair service for broken farming implements which had been leading to delays in ploughing. The barefoot builders' schemes were popular with communities which needed, for one reason or another, to build their own houses on a massive scale and the handpump mechanics' scheme responded to the community's need for reduced dependence on unreliable government maintenance teams.

A third and related factor is that of concentrating on a specific need which has been identified by the beneficiaries as a priority, rather than launching immediately into complex integrated programmes. For example, the success of the Grameen Bank in Bangladesh is partly attributed to the fact that it started with the most immediate need of the rural landless — credit — and only later started to add on other components.

A fourth factor is the extent to which agency staff and trainers have tried to learn from and include trainees and communities in the design and implementation of training courses. By and large, this has resulted in training which is appropriate in terms of content, level, length and location and which incorporates concern for and is based on local conditions and culture.

The issue of accountability is also an important one. Many of the case studies put this forward as a factor which led to the success of community-based services. Generally, workers paid by distant government officials are less industrious than those paid by the community. In part, this is because the community workers are concerned about respect. In some cases, such as the handpump mechanics in India, poor performance means no pay, and the community also has the right to withhold payment altogether and choose someone else to go for training.

Account must also be taken of the type of agencies which have promoted barefoot service schemes. Many are NGOs which have a very strong commitment to the concept of helping the poor to help themselves. This degree of commitment, as well as the in-depth knowledge of rural communities which is needed to design effective grassroots level programmes, can sometimes be found in government-initiated schemes, for example with the original barefoot doctors' scheme in China. For the main part, however, the successful attempts at copying and promoting the barefoot concept have been initiated by NGOs.

Prospects for expansion and replication

Given their limited resources, the heavy involvement of NGOs in the barefoot approach to development raises questions as to how many people can be expected to benefit from the provision of appropriate rural services in the near future.

Only a few of the case studies indicate how the pilot schemes described are likely to be expanded or replicated elsewhere. The case study on vets in Gujarat talks about the interest of other agencies in India and in Kenya in replicating the approach. The case study of builders in Iran explains how the first group of trainees themselves organized training for a new group of trainees to whom they passed on their knowledge. The Botswana case study describes how blacksmiths will be enabled to set up 'mini-centres' to pass on the fruits of their training to others and, of course, the Grameen Bank example from Bangladesh is within itself an example of how a pilot project benefiting a handful of people has, with support from the government and massive donor support, been expanded to cover many thousands more.

The projects described in the case studies give an encouraging glimpse of what is possible with a 'people first' approach to the provision of rural services. What is needed now is a concerted effort on behalf of NGOs, governments and donors to work with each other and together with rural communities to replicate such programmes on a widespread basis.

REFERENCES

Doctors in China — the origins of the barefoot approach

Horn, J S (1969). *'Away with all pests.....' An English surgeon in People's China*, Paul Hamlyn, London/New York/Sydney/Toronto.

Morely, D, Rohde, J and Williams, G (eds) (1983). *Practising health for all*, Oxford University Press, Oxford.

Economists in Ecuador and Nepal

Agricultural Development Bank (1984), 'Highlights on Small Farmer Development Programme in Nepal', ADBN, Kathmandu.

Esman, M J et al (1980). 'Paraprofessionals in Rural Development', Cornell University, Ithaca.

Maharjan, K H (1987). 'Peoples' participation in an irrigation project', Agricultural Credit 16, ACTI, Kathmandu.

Malla, P H (1986). 'A case study on group fishery project of SFDP Mahnedranagar, Dhanusha', Agricultural Credit 15, ACTI, Kathmandu.

Max-Neef, M (1982). *From the Outside Looking In: Experiences in 'barefoot economics'*, Dag Hammerskjold Foundation, Uppsala.

Oakley, P and Marsden, D (1984). 'Approaches to Participation in Rural Development', ILO, Geneva.

Uphoff, N (1985). 'Fitting projects to people', *Putting People First: Sociological variables in rural development*, Cernea M M (ed), World Bank/OUP.

Village artisans in Botswana

Village Artisan Training Manual, (1982). Rural Industries Promotions, Botswana.

Catalogue of RIIC Goods and Services, (1985). Rural Industries Promotions, Botswana.

Annual Report, (1986). Rural Industries Promotions, Botswana.

Builders in Iran, Guinea and the Sudan

1. Development Workshop is an international non-profit organization working in the field of human settlements in less developed countries. The group strives to improve the ability of communities and governments of less developed countries to meet their needs of shelter, physical infrastructure and planning, and believes in developing the use of local skills and resources. Development Workshop can be contacted at Box 133, 238 Davenport Road, Toronto M5R 1J6, Canada or BP 10, Montayral, 47500 Fumel, France.
2. A training programme for staff from the Directorate of Housing and Construction, the Department of Community Development and local employees of aid agencies, all concerned with community development and building. Core sponsorship for the programme was provided by EuroAction Acord.
3. This occurred following two of the three programmes described here, with a 'Manuel de construction parasismique en Guinee' by John Norton, Development Workshop, 1986, and for Southern Sudan, a 'Manual for constructing a community building' by John Norton, 1st edition EuroAction Acord; 2nd edition Development Workshop, 1986.

Geologists in Sri Lanka

Ajakaiye, D C and Woakes, M (1983). 'Training of Applied Geoscientists in Africa', Proc Reg Workshop, *Role of Geoscience Educational Institutes in National Resources Development in Africa*, CIFEG Occas. Publ 1983/1, p.10-14.

Brock, (1975). 'Geoscientists and the Third World', in Berger, A R (ed), *Geological Survey of Canada, Paper 74-57*, 32pp.

Carman, J S (1983). 'Training with Particular Reference to the Needs of Small Mines', in Woakes, M and Carman, J S (eds), *AGID Guide to Mineral Resources Development*, AGID Rept 10, Bangkok, p.47-55.

Chesworth, W, Marias-Vazquez, F, Acquaye, D and Thompson, E (1983). 'Agricultural alchemy: Stones into Bread', *Episodes*, 1, p.3-7.

Chesworth, W, Van Straaten, P, Semoka, M R and Mchihiyo, E P (1985). Agrogeology in Tanzania, *Episodes*, 8, 4, p.257-8.

Cooray, P G (ed), (1977). *Geoscience Education in Developing Countries*, AGID Rept 5, Bangkok, 56pp.

Cooray, P G (1984). 'The Geosciences and Resource Development in Sri Lanka', *Pangea*, 3, p.38-41.

Davies, D (1975). 'Earthquake Prediction in China', *Nature*, 258, p.286-7.

Freemantle, M (1983). The Poor World needs Chemists, *New Scientist*, 28, p.226-9.

Friedman, Y (1984). 'Don't make new deserts...'. *UNU Newsletter*, 8, 1, p.4-5.

Katz, M B (1982). 'Relevance in University Earth Science Aid to Developing Countries', 24th Int Geol Congr Montreal, Symp 2, p.182-6.

Legga, C A (1982). 'The Role of the Zambian Geological Survey in Small Mines Development', in Neilson, J M (ed) *Strategies for Small Scale Mining and Mineral Industries*, AGID Rept 8, Bangkok, p.70-77.

Martin, W J (1982). 'Education of Middle Level Earth Science Manpower in East Africa', in Neilson, J M (ed) *Strategies for Small Scale Mining and Mineral Industries*, AGID Rept 8, Bangkok, p.171-6.

Mazimhaka, P K (1982). 'The Role of Small Deposits in Uganda's Mineral Production', in Neilson, J M (ed) *Strategies for Small Scale Mining and Mineral Industries*, AGID Rept 8, Bangkok, p.61-70.

Meyer, R F and Carman, J S (eds) (1980). *The Future of Small Scale Mining*, McGraw Hill, UNITAR, New York.

Minato, H (1983). 'Some Problems in the Development of Small-Scale Mines — The Case of Non-Metallic Mining', *Role of Geosciences in Development*, Proc UNU-Tokyo Geog Soc Symp 1981, p.89-94.

Moravcsik, M and Exell, H B (1978). 'Third World needs "Barefoot" Sciences', *Nature* 276, p.315-6.

Neilson, J M (ed) (1982). *Strategies for Small Scale Mining and Mineral Industries*, AGID Rept 8, Bangkok, 199pp.

Richardson, D S (1982). 'Small Scale Mining of Gypsum at Mkomazi, Tanzania', in Neilson, J M (ed). *Strategies for Small Scale Mining and Mineral Industries*, AGID Rept 8, Bangkok, p.112-20.

Salas, G P (1983). 'Mineral Exploration and Exploitation (Small Scale Mining)', *Role of Geosciences in Development*, Proc UNU-Tokyo Geog Soc Symp 1981, p.85-88.

Shimazaki, Y (1983). 'Problems related to the Training of Professional Geoscientists with Particular Reference to Mineral Resources Evaluation', *Role of Geosciences in Development*, Proc UNU-Tokyo Geog Soc Symp 1981, p.135-9.

Stigzielius, Ho (1980). 'Small Scale Mining in Finland' in Meyer, R F and Carman, J S (eds). *The Future of Small Scale Mining*, McGraw Hill, UNITAR, New York, p.249-51.

UN (1970). 'Mineral Resources Development with particular reference to the Developing Countries'. Dept Economics and Social Affairs, New York.

UN (1972). 'Small-Scale Mining in the Developing Countries', Dept Economics and Social Affairs, New York.

Wels, T A (1983). 'Small Scale Mining — The Forgotten Partners', Trans

Inst Min Metal Sect A, p.19-27.

Wise, M J (1983). 'Education and Development', *Role of Geosciences in Development*, Proc UNU-Tokyo Geog Soc Symp 1981, p.128-34.

ALSO FROM IT PUBLICATIONS

Microenterprises in Developing Countries
Edited by Jacob Levitsky

Microenterprises are in many respects the most crucial and dynamic part of the economies of most developing countries. This collection of 16 papers outlines ways to enhance the effectiveness of microenterprise in contributing to the general development of the Third World, and to the search for a widespread improvement in living standards.

272pp   ISBN 1 85339 016 X   paperback

**Blacksmith, Baker, Roofing-sheet Maker . . .
Employment for rural women in developing countries**
Marilyn Carr

A source of ideas for all those who are helping develop cash-producing work for Third World women. It uses over 50 case studies to show how less conventional projects have developed the earning power of women in more competitive fields of activity; the evidence is taken from 22 countries and covers 38 trades.

158pp   ISBN 0 946688 15 X   paperback

These titles are available through *Books by Post*, which contains details of a selection of recommended titles on Appropriate Technology and Development issues, from publishers throughout the world, annotated to help those ordering by mail. Write for a copy of *Books by Post* or visit the **IT Bookshop** at 103/105 Southampton Row, London WC1B 4HH, UK.

www.ingramcontent.com/pod-product-compliance
Ingram Content Group UK Ltd.
Pitfield, Milton Keynes, MK11 3LW, UK
UKHW021846140426
5217IPUK00022B/1627